HOW TO BUILD

BOOKCASES & BOOKSHELVES

15 Woodworking Projects for Book Lovers

Edited by Scott Francis

POPULAR WOODWORKING BOOKS

CINCINNATI, OHIO

popularwoodworking.com

HOW TO BUILD

BOOKCASES & BOOKSHELVES

15 Woodworking Projects for Book Lovers

Edited by Scott Francis

CONTENTS

BOOK DISPLAYS

INTRODUCTION

Who invented the bookcase? It's a question that countless furniture designers, carpenters and bibliophiles would love to know the answer to. Unfortunately the answer is a mystery – likely because like books themselves, the method of storing them has evolved slowly over time.

The history of bookcases is intertwined with the evolution of the written word, the invention of the printing press and the development of books with spines. Books, of course, weren't always books as we know them. Texts were rolled up as scrolls or sheaves of paper bound up with bands of leather. They were kept in trunks, chained to desks, stacked in piles on the floor and stored using a variety of methods throughout history. Books were even shelved with their spines facing the back of shelves – titles or identifying marks appeared on the outward facing pages.

Most of these early book collections were kept by the clergy, administrative bodies or the wealthy. As these libraries amassed various storage solutions were explored. Early bookshelves evolved from cupboards. Texts were typically stacked flat on the shelves. French cabinetmaker André-Charles Boulle is often credited with designing the first low bookcase. With a marble top and doors with silk curtains, the bookcase was approximately 4 feet high by 5 feet. As the evolution of books progressed, spines faced out and books were displayed instead of simply kept. Doors became used less frequently and the bookcase as we know it began to come into focus.

The introduction of the printing press to the western world by Johannes Guttenberg around 1440 gave rise to more personal book collections and private libraries. Built in shelving as well as standing pieces of furniture dedicated to storing books became popular around the 1700s. English diarist Samuel Pepys is credited with commissioning the earliest tall bookcases in the 1660s as he sought a solution for his growing library, which included more than 3,000 books.

Today, unless you have no soul, it is difficult to look at a bookcase filled with volumes and not feel a deep connection to history and scholarly pursuits. Who doesn't love opening a volume and smelling that old book smell? There's something tactile in that experience that can never be replaced by reading something on screen. For those who crave that tangible relationship with their books, what better way to honor that connection than to build your own bookcases to house them? Your personal library will be all the more special when you can look at the shelving you've created for it and know you made it yourself.

This book – which will hopefully one day rest on a shelf you've built – discusses 13 bookcases based on various designs seen throughout the history of furniture making as well as a couple of smaller book displays for your desk.

Enjoy.

TECHNIQUES

CHAPTER ONE

Build Better Bookcases

by Robert W. Lang

Everyone needs a bookcase, and if you're a beginning woodworker, it's a great project to develop skills without breaking the bank. So what makes the ideal bookcase? It should fit in the average home, look good and be made to last. Here we also wanted to show that the same basic construction could be dressed up in different ways to suit anyone's sense of style. What follows is a plan that makes good use of materials, and is relatively quick and easy to put together and finish.

Basic Bookcase Construction

The basic cabinet is built from one 4' by 8' sheet of ¾"-thick hardwood plywood plus a few board feet of solid wood. This keeps the cost reasonable, but introduces some constraints on the size of the finished bookcase. Our final design is 5' high and a little less than 2½'-wide. It's not quite as deep as many bookcases, but it is a useful size for all but the largest books. It does its job without taking over the room, will hold a lot of books and the shelves won't sag. You can make the basic design any size you want, but if you make it larger you won't be able to get all of the parts from one sheet of plywood. If you make it wider, keep the shelves less than 36". If the shelves are longer than that, they will likely sag when loaded with books.

Using ¾" plywood for the back as well as the other cabinet parts produces a box that is very strong. The edges of the plywood are all covered with solid wood. In three of the four designs this is a face frame applied to the front of the box. The other design uses ¼"-thick hardwood as an edge band.

I used biscuit joints to hold the case together and pocket screws to join the face frames. The assembled face frame is glued to the front of the cabinet. There is enough surface area for a good joint, without nail holes showing in the completed cabinet.

Using plywood solves many problems you would have if you made the bookcase from solid wood; the grain and color of all the parts will be similar, you won't have to glue any parts together for width and seasonal wood movement won't be an issue.

The Trouble with Plywood

Plywood however, does introduce some problems that you need to be aware of. The veneer face is very thin. You need to handle it carefully to avoid scratching it, and when you sand you need to be careful that you don't sand through the veneer. Despite what some people might tell you, the factory edges are not straight, and you should never assume that the corners of the sheet are square.

The other problem with plywood is its thickness. It will be between 1/32" and 1/16" less than ¾", and the thickness can vary throughout the sheet. If you cut the horizontal parts to the dimensions in the cutting list, your cabinet will finish slightly smaller in width. If you then cut the top and make the face frame to the listed size, they won't quite fit. The first thing you need to do is determine the actual thickness. Then develop a strategy for working around this discrepancy.

I began by crosscutting the plywood at 60", as shown in the cutting diagram. This large piece will yield the two long sides of the bookcase and the back. The smaller piece will provide the top and bottom of the cabinet, as well as the fixed and adjustable shelves. There is a little

One of the most important facts about plywood is that it is almost always thinner than the stated dimension. This (one of four types) ¾" plywood was 1/32" undersized.

SHAKER
Made from cherry plywood with a solid cherry face frame. The profiles for the mouldings were taken from typical details used in original Shaker pieces.

CONTEMPORARY
Made without a face frame from maple plywood with ¼"-thick solid maple glued and nailed to the raw edges of the plywood.

ARTS & CRAFTS
Quartersawn white oak plywood and solid wood were used to construct the Arts & Crafts bookcase. The beveled mouldings were typical on built-in bookcases and other cabinets of the early 20th century.

FORMAL
The most complex bookcase is made from African mahogany plywood, with genuine mahogany face frame and mouldings. Additional mouldings are applied to the side to form panels.

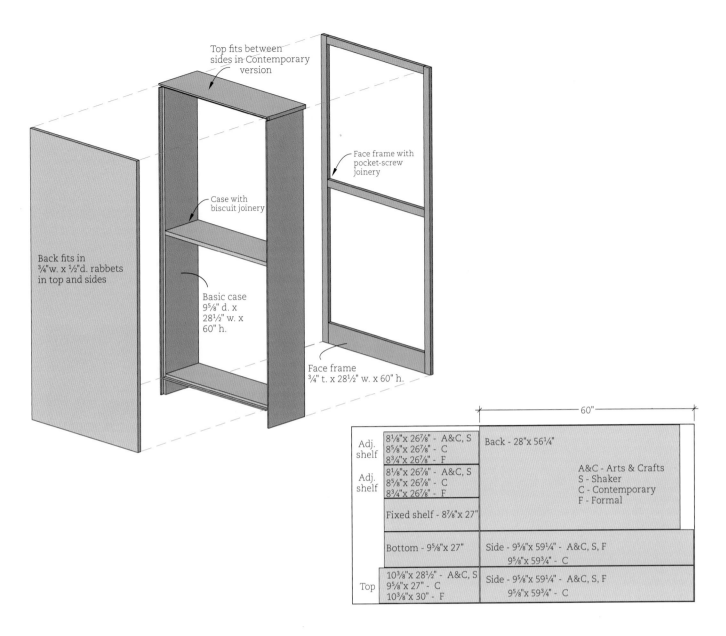

Top fits between sides in Contemporary version

Face frame with pocket-screw joinery

Case with biscuit joinery

Back fits in ¾"w. x ½"d. rabbets in top and sides

Basic case 9⅝" d. x 28½" w. x 60" h.

Face frame ¾" t. x 28½" w. x 60" h.

— 60" —

Adj. shelf	8⅛"x 26⅞" - A&C, S 8⅝"x 26⅞" - C 8¾"x 26⅞" - F	Back - 28"x 56¼"
Adj. shelf	8⅛"x 26⅞" - A&C, S 8⅝"x 26⅞" - C 8¾"x 26⅞" - F	A&C - Arts & Crafts S - Shaker C - Contemporary F - Formal
	Fixed shelf - 8⅞"x 27"	
	Bottom - 9⅝"x 27"	Side - 9⅝"x 59¼" - A&C, S, F 9⅝"x 59¾" - C
Top	10⅜"x 28½" - A&C, S 9⅝"x 27" - C 10⅜"x 30" - F	Side - 9⅝"x 59¼" - A&C, S, F 9⅝"x 59¾" - C

extra room to allow for squaring the ends of the finished parts and cutting clean long edges. You can make this crosscut on the table saw, but it's easier to cut the full sheet with a circular saw and a straightedge. You could also make this first cut with a jigsaw, and then clean up the edge with a router. If you go this route, clamp a straightedge to the sheet, make sure it's square and run a flush trimming bit against it to clean up the cut.

Make the first rip cut on the table saw ¼" wider than the finished part. Then move the fence in to trim the opposite edge. Keep the best side up, and the freshly cut edges against the fence so that you have two clean edges on each part. After ripping, I crosscut the parts on a sliding compound miter saw, using a stop to make sure that pairs of parts were the exact same length, which is important.

The plywood I was using was ¹⁄₃₂" thinner than ¾", so I made the parts that go between the sides ¹⁄₁₆" longer than the listed length. This allows the cabinet to finish at the correct width.

Develop a Strategy

Look at the exploded drawing above to understand how the parts of the basic carcase go together. The back sits in a ¾"-wide by ½"-deep rabbet cut in the back edges of the sides, the bottom and the top. In the three versions with face frames, the bottom and fixed shelf go between the cabinet sides, and the top sits on the upper edge of the sides. In the contemporary bookcase, one difference is that the top goes between the sides.

The fixed middle shelf is ¾" narrower than the cabinet bottom so its back edge is even with the rabbet in the other parts. The top is ¾" wider than the bottom, as the front edge covers the top of the face frame.

Cut the parts from the sheet of plywood in stages. I cut only the two sides, the bottom and the fixed shelf to

Story stick

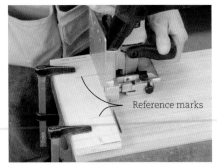

Reference marks

The rabbet at the back edge of the cabinet sides, bottom and top is made with a stack dado set on the table saw. The featherboard holds the plywood down flat to the surface of the saw.

The story stick, made from a scrap of plywood shows all of the cabinet parts at full size. Make one and put away your tape measure. Use it to lay out all of the parts quickly and accurately.

A second story stick acts as a jig to locate the biscuit slots in the cabinet sides. Reference marks for the slots line up with the centerline on the bottom of the machine.

Speed square

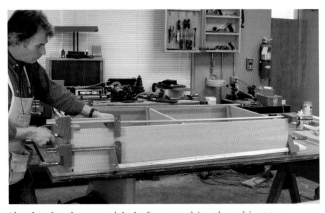

With the cabinet on its side, I can easily reach both the front and back edges to keep them flush. Speed squares clamped to the side and shelves keep the cabinet square during this glue-up.

I let the glue dry overnight before attaching the cabinet top. Because the top is placed above the cabinet sides I had to use clamps in pairs to hold the top down as shown here.

final size before assembling the box. I then cut the top to the right width, and cut its rabbet in the back with the other parts, but I left it long until after the basic box was assembled.

If something went wrong with one of these parts, I could make them into adjustable shelves, and replace them with the parts from the remaining plywood. This is less efficient than cutting all the parts at once, but it's insurance against mistakes.

I cut the rabbet with a stack dado set in the table saw, using a featherboard to hold the stock down (as shown above). Plywood is often bowed, and if it raises up while it is going across the dado stack, the rabbet won't be a consistent depth. Making the rabbet ½" deep gives room to attach the back with # 6 x 1⅝" screws.

Making Layout Simple

With the carcase parts cut and rabbeted, I took a 60"-long piece of scrap plywood and made a story stick, showing at full scale the positions of the plywood parts, as well as the parts for the face frame. The most likely

place to make a mistake is in measuring, and the story stick transfers the locations to the finished parts without measuring.

I also made a second story stick, 3¼" wide by 10⅜". This was used to locate the slots for the biscuits in the cabinet sides, and in the edges of the bottom piece and the fixed shelf. I clamped this to the bottom edge of the cabinet sides, placed the bottom of the biscuit joiner against the marks and cut the slots.

To set the height of the cutter for the slots in the ends of the shelves, I placed a shelf flat on the bench, set the biscuit joiner next to it, and lowered the fence until it was flush with the top surface of the shelf. This indexes the machine so the slots cut using the guide block line up with the slots cut using the machine's fence.

With all the joints ready, it's tempting to go ahead and glue the cabinet together. It is faster, and you get a better finish if at this point you finish sand all of the inside surfaces, then assemble.

Arts & Crafts Style

The Arts & Crafts bookcase and the Shaker book-case are constructed the same way. I assembled the cabinet with one side across two sawhorses. This let me position clamps across both sides of each joint. I clamped a speed square on each of two opposite corners to keep the box square while the glue dried.

Before attaching the top, I still needed to cut it to its exact length. Instead of relying on the cutting list, I checked the outside dimension of the assembled box to be certain to get a good fit without the undersized plywood throwing me off. I held the top in place against the ends of the sides and made a couple of marks for the biscuits. To clamp the top in position, I had to hook two clamps together as shown on page 12.

Before attaching the face frame, sand the front edges flush with a flat sanding block. I used a cloth-backed sanding belt glued to plywood.

With the stiles clamped to the assembled box, I mark both the length and the exact location of the rails directly. This eliminates errors due to measuring or using undersized plywood.

The face frame is put together with pocket screws before being glued in place on the assembled cabinet box. Two clamps hold the stile on edge so that I can see and reach both sides of the joint.

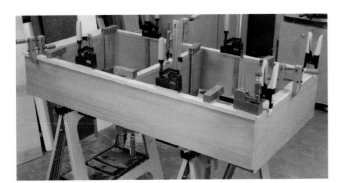

It might take every clamp you own, plus a few borrowed from a neighbor, to attach the face frame. It's worth the effort to get it lined up perfectly without leaving nail holes to be filled.

It's safer to trim the solid wood parts down to the plywood parts. The block plane works quickly against an edge or against the veneer.

A card scraper brings the solid wood even with the plywood without raising a cloud of dust, or risking the damage that a belt sander or random-orbit sander could cause.

I put together the basic box with the bottom and fixed shelf between the sides, and the top of the cabinet above the sides. Before working on the face frame, I made sure that all the edges on the cabinet were flush by sanding them with a sanding block. It's simply a piece of plywood 3" wide with a piece of a sanding belt glued to it. By holding it flat on two adjacent surfaces, any variations can be quickly removed so that the face frame will sit flat.

The face frame is assembled and glued to the front edge of the plywood box. The outside edges of the face frame are flush with the outside faces of the plywood when the cabinet is complete, but you want to make the face frame so that it extends slightly beyond the veneer. If you try to make it dead flush you are likely to end up with the veneer proud of the solid wood frame at some point. If this happens it's almost impossible to correct without sanding through the thin veneer.

Put Your Tape Away

Instead of measuring the parts for the face frame, I put the assembled cabinet on its back, and clamped the stiles to the front edges of the plywood, letting the long edges hang over the plywood about 1⁄32". Then I marked the length and the location of the rails directly from the plywood parts. Once the rails are the correct length, I used a pocket-hole jig to drill holes in the ends of each rail.

After assembling the face frame, it is glued down to the plywood. It takes a lot of clamps to get a nice tight glue line. The face frame can be nailed down, but that means filling all the holes.

Where Solid Meets Ply

After letting the glue on the face-frame-to-cabinet joint dry overnight, it was time to clean up where the plywood and solid wood meet. Because the solid wood was proud of the veneer, I could use a block plane and scraper to bring the surfaces flush.

In the past I've used a random-orbit sander or belt sander for this task, but I have found

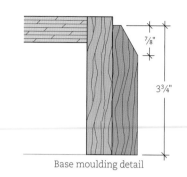

Base moulding detail

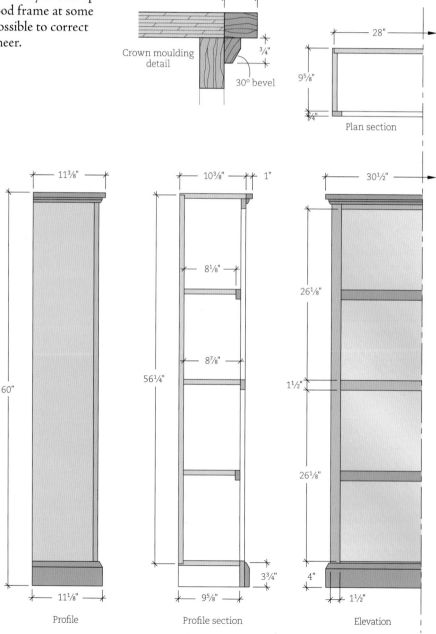

Crown moulding detail

Plan section

Profile

Profile section

Elevation

that using the plane and card scraper is faster, does a better job and there is a lot less risk of going through the plywood's thin face veneer.

The trim around the front and sides of the plywood cabinet top is mitered at the corners, and glued to the edges. If these trim pieces are bowed, I use a few biscuits to help keep the solid wood flush with the plywood.

I glued the solid-wood edges to the two adjustable shelves, and then bored the holes for the adjustable shelf pins using a jig I made, shown on page 16. You may need to trim the shelves to fit behind the face frame. I then sanded everything inside and out to #240-grit to prepare it for finishing.

The crown and base mouldings for the Arts & Crafts cabinet are made with 30° bevel cuts. I made the cuts on the table saw and then removed the saw marks with my block plane.

The Arts & Crafts finish consists of General Finishes' Java gel stain, followed by amber shellac. After a coat of wax, I put the back in place, attaching it with #6 x 1⅝" screws.

Arts & Crafts-Style Bookcase

NO.	ITEM	DIMENSIONS (INCHES)			MATERIAL	COMMENTS
		T	W	L		
2	Sides	¾"	9⅝"	59¼"	Plywood	QSWO*
1	Bottom	¾"	9⅝"	27"	Plywood	QSWO
1	Fixed shelf	¾"	8⅞"	27"	Plywood	QSWO
1	Top	¾"	10⅜"	28½"	Plywood	QSWO
1	Back	¾"	28"	56¼"	Plywood	QSWO
2	Adj. shelves	¾"	8⅛"	26⅞"	Plywood	QSWO
2	Stiles	¾"	1½"	59¼"	Solid	QSWO
2	Rails	¾"	1½"	25½"	Solid	QSWO
1	Bottom rail	¾"	4"	25½"	Solid	QSWO
2	Shelf edges	¾"	1½"	26⅞"	Solid	QSWO
1	Top trim	¾"	1"	60"	Solid	QSWO
1	Top trim	½"	¾"	60"	Solid	QSWO
1	Base trim	¾"	3¾"	60"	Solid	QSWO

*Quartersawn white oak

Shaker Style

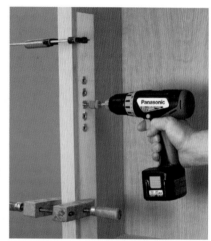

The Shaker bookcase is assembled and trimmed in the same way as the Arts & Crafts case. The only difference between the two is the profile of the mouldings, the species of wood and the finish.

All of these mouldings were made on the router table. The bullnose trim around the top of the cabinet can be made with two passes over a ⅜"-radius quarter-round bit, or one pass over a bullnose cutter. Either way, leave a slight flat spot at the center of the radius. If you machine off the entire curve, the wood will move toward the router bit at the end of the cut and leave a snipe in the last few inches of the moulding.

The cove moulding starts as a ¾" x ¾" piece of square stock. The ⅝" radius was milled on the router table. The base moulding is a ½"-radius bead with the cutter set to be flush with the face of the moulding at one end, leaving a ¼" x ⅛" step at the top edge. Use a pair of feather-boards to hold the stock down to the router table and tight to the fence while making the mouldings. Make one pass to remove most of the waste, and then reset the router to make a final, light finishing pass.

Apply the Trim

Putting the trim around the edges of the top is the most exacting part of this project. I added an auxiliary fence and table to my miter saw, as shown on page 20 and I then made a 45° cut in each direction so that I would have a reference to exactly where the cut would be made. I marked the cuts directly from the assembled cabinet and lined up the marks to the kerf in the auxiliary fence and table.

After I made the mouldings on the router table, I cut the pieces of trim a few inches longer than needed. I then made a 45° cut on one end of each of the three pieces. This let me check the angle at the corners. I held one end of the front piece against one of the short legs, and then marked

the other end by running my pencil across the back of it, where it met the side of the cabinet. I usually make the cut just a little long, check the angle with the mating piece and then make the final cut.

The trim is glued to the cabinet, no nails are necessary. I trimmed the top first, and then scraped the top edge flush with the veneer.

The Shaker cabinet is finished with Watco Danish oil. I wanted to add a bit of color to the wood so I mixed half medium walnut and half natural together, and applied two coats of oil followed by one coat of paste wax.

I used a shop-made jig to drill the holes for the pegs for the adjustable shelves. ¼"-20 T-nuts act as bushings to guide a brad-point drill bit. After drilling the holes for the T-nuts on 1" centers top-to-bottom, I used a twist drill bit to bore out the soft threads in the T-nuts, leaving a ¼" diameter.

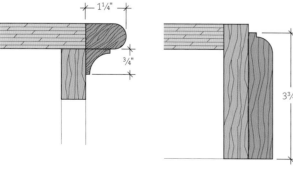
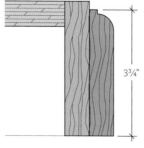

Crown moulding detail   Base moulding detail

Shaker-Style Bookcase

NO.	ITEM	DIMENSIONS (INCHES)			MATERIAL	COMMENTS
		T	W	L		
2	Sides	¾"	9⅝"	59¼"	Plywood	Cherry
1	Bottom	¾"	9⅝"	27"	Plywood	Cherry
1	Fixed shelf	¾"	8⅞"	27"	Plywood	Cherry
1	Top	¾"	10⅜"	28½"	Plywood	Cherry
1	Back	¾"	28"	56¼"	Plywood	Cherry
2	Adj. shelves	¾"	8⅛"	26⅞"	Plywood	Cherry
2	Stiles	¾"	1½"	59¼"	Solid	Cherry
2	Rails	¾"	1½"	25½"	Solid	Cherry
1	Bottom rail	¾"	4"	25½"	Solid	Cherry
2	Shelf edges	¾"	1½"	26⅞"	Solid	Cherry
1	Top trim	¾"	1¼"	60"	Solid	Cherry
1	Top trim	¾"	¾"	60"	Solid	Cherry
1	Base trim	¾"	3¾"	60"	Solid	Cherry

Contemporary Style

This bookcase is made without a face frame. It is lighter and simpler in appearance, and takes less time to build and finish. Instead of a face frame, the visible front edges of the plywood are covered with ¼"-thick strips of solid wood.

The plywood sides of this cabinet are cut to a finished length of 59¾" and a piece of edge trim is put on the ends before the front trim is applied. The top piece in this version is the same size as the bottom, and fits in between the sides. Because of this, the basic cabinet carcase should be assembled in one step.

Trim Now, Assemble Later

The solid edges are applied and trimmed before the cabinet box is put together. I ripped the strips to ⅜" and then took them down to ¼" thick by making two passes through the planer. The solid maple I used had been planed to 1⁄32" over ¾", so the strips were about 1⁄16" wider than the plywood was thick. This extra width makes it easy to attach the strips without worrying about lining up the edge of the solid wood perfectly.

I trimmed the solid wood down to the level of the plywood with a block plane followed by a card scraper. You could use a router with a flush-trimming bit, but it's awkward to try to balance the base of the router on the edge of the piece. If the router tilts at all, the bit will dig in and ruin the edge. The router bit will also likely tear out a piece of the solid wood if the grain direction isn't consistent.

Assemble the box after applying the edges. Below the bottom shelf is a 3¼"- high, 27"-wide (grain runs vertically) piece of plywood to support the bottom shelf. The face of this kick board piece is set in ¼" from the edge of the cabinet sides. I finished the bookcase with Minwax Polycrylic Semigloss clear finish.

I clamped each part vertically on the bench to attach the edges with glue and 23-gauge pins. The edges are wider than the plywood is thick.

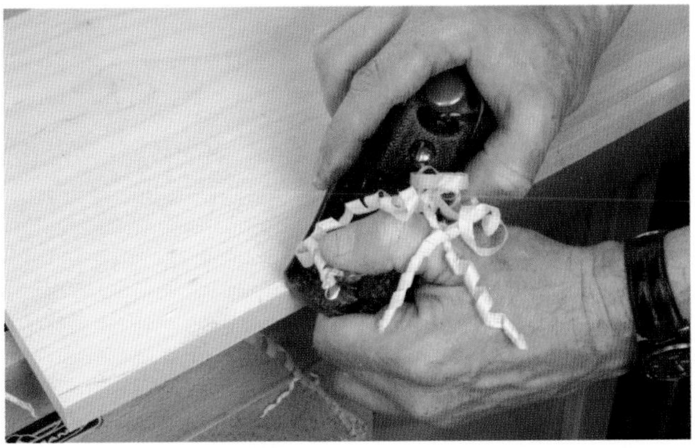

Before assembling the cabinet, trim the solid wood edges flush to the plywood using a block plane followed by a card scraper. I sanded all the parts before assembly.

Contemporary-Style Bookcase

NO.	ITEM	DIMENSIONS (INCHES) T	W	L	MATERIAL	COMMENTS
2	Sides	¾"	9⅝"	59¾"	Plywood	Maple
2	Top & bottom	¾"	9⅝"	27"	Plywood	Maple
1	Fixed shelf	¾"	8⅞"	27"	Plywood	Maple
2	Adj. shelves	¾"	8⅛"	26⅞"	Plywood	Maple
1	Back	¾"	28"	56¼"	Plywood	Maple
1	Kick board	¾"	27"	3¾"	Plywood	Maple
1	Edge trim	¼"	2 5⁄32"	30LF*	Solid	Maple

*Linear feet

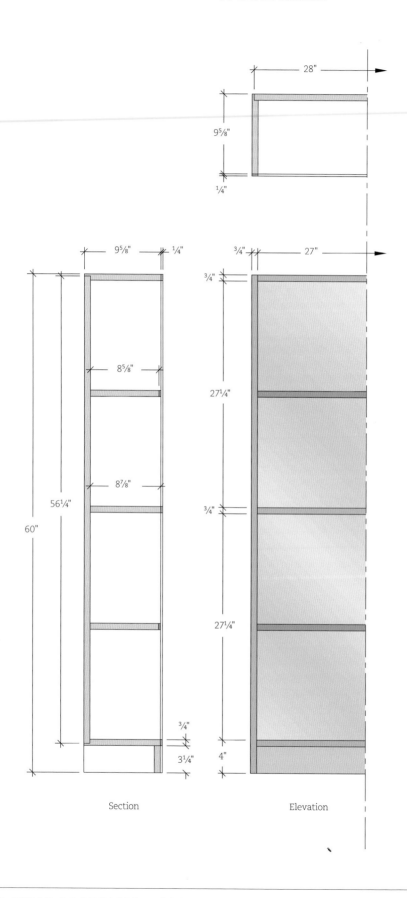

Section

Elevation

Formal Style

The plywood case of the formal cabinet is assembled the same way as the other two face-frame cabinets, but the top and the face frame are both larger to accommodate the paneled trim on the outside of the bookcase. The shelves are also deeper. Instead of tucking behind the face frame, they sit ⅛" back from the front of the face frame.

The edge of the face frame is flush with the inside edge of the cabinet side instead of the outside. This allows for the addition of pieces of solid wood on the outside of the cabinet to look like paneling. The top also overhangs the side of the cabinet ¾" so that it is above the paneling. The joint between the two is covered by the crown moulding.

Make the face-frame stiles ¹⁹/₁₆" wide so that the edges of the face frame are proud of the veneer on both the inside of the cabinet, and the panel stiles on the outside. If you need to trim or sand after everything is put together, it's better to trim and sand these narrow edges.

Applied Paneling

With the cabinet box assembled, and the face frame in place, I marked the locations of the applied stiles and rails on the face of the plywood. The front stile fits behind the edge of the face frame and is only 1¼" wide. The stile at the back edge is 2" wide, equal to the width of the front stile added to the thickness of the face frame.

The 2"-wide middle rail is centered vertically on the side of the cabinet. The top and bottom rails are made to leave 2" exposed from the edge of the crown and base mouldings. This makes the top rail 3¼" wide. I made the bottom rail the same width, and added a piece of 1½"-wide material to the bottom edge of the cabinet side for attaching the base moulding.

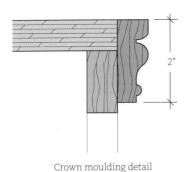

Crown moulding detail

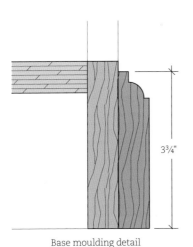

Base moulding detail

Formal-Style Bookcase

NO.	ITEM	DIMENSIONS (INCHES)			MATERIAL	COMMENTS
		T	W	L		
2	Sides	¾"	9⅝"	59¼"	Plywood	Mahogany
1	Bottom	¾"	9⅝"	27"	Plywood	Mahogany
1	Fixed shelf	¾"	8⅞"	27"	Plywood	Mahogany
1	Top	¾"	10⅜"	30"	Plywood	Mahogany
1	Back	¾"	28"	56¼"	Plywood	Mahogany
2	Adj. shelves	¾"	8¾"	26⅞"	Plywood	Mahogany
2	FF stiles	¾"	1⁹/₁₆"	59¼"	Solid	Mahogany
2	FF rails	¾"	1½"	27"	Solid	Mahogany
1	FF bottom rail	¾"	4"	27"	Solid	Mahogany
2	Shelf edges	¾"	1½"	26⅞"	Solid	Mahogany
2	Front cab stile	¾"	1¼"	59¼"	Solid	Mahogany
2	Back cab stile	¾"	2"	59¼"	Solid	Mahogany
2	Cab top rail	¾"	3¼"	6⅜"	Solid	Mahogany
2	Cab middle rail	¾"	2"	6⅜"	Solid	Mahogany
2	Cab bottom rail	¾"	3¼"	6⅜"	Solid	Mahogany
1	Cab bead moulding	½"	¹¹/₁₆"	28LF	Solid	Mahogany
1	Cab cove moulding	½"	½"	28LF	Solid	Mahogany
1	Crown moulding	¾"	2"	60"	Solid	Mahogany
1	Base moulding	¾"	3¾"	60"	Solid	Mahogany

After laying out the locations of the stiles and rails, I glued and clamped the solid-wood parts to the plywood cabinet sides. An extra piece of wood is added at the bottom edge of the cabinet to support the short leg of the base moulding.

By holding the gun upside down, and pulling the trigger with my little finger, I can nail the bead moulding from the side. The next layer of moulding will cover the holes.

Attaching a sacrificial base and fence to the miter saw lets me see precisely where the cut will be made by lining up my pencil marks with the saw kerfs.

The solid wood stiles and rails, combined with the bead, cove and crown mouldings are a simple way to produce a rich paneled look to the finished bookcase.

I used glue only to hold these in place, clamping them down and letting the glue dry for an hour. Then I began applying the trim to the inside edges. I marked the lengths of the mitered pieces directly from the corners of the stiles and rails.

Two-step Moulding

The bead moulding can be nailed from the side, because the cove moulding will cover the nail holes. I fit and placed all the bead moulding before beginning to fit the cove. I did nail the cove moulding with 23-gauge pins. These leave very tiny holes that I filled with a bit of sanding dust mixed with clear lacquer.

After all the panel moulding was on, I cut and fit the crown, and after a final sanding stained the wood with Behlen's "American Walnut" NGR stain, followed by two coats of shellac.

FORMAL-STYLE BOOKCASE

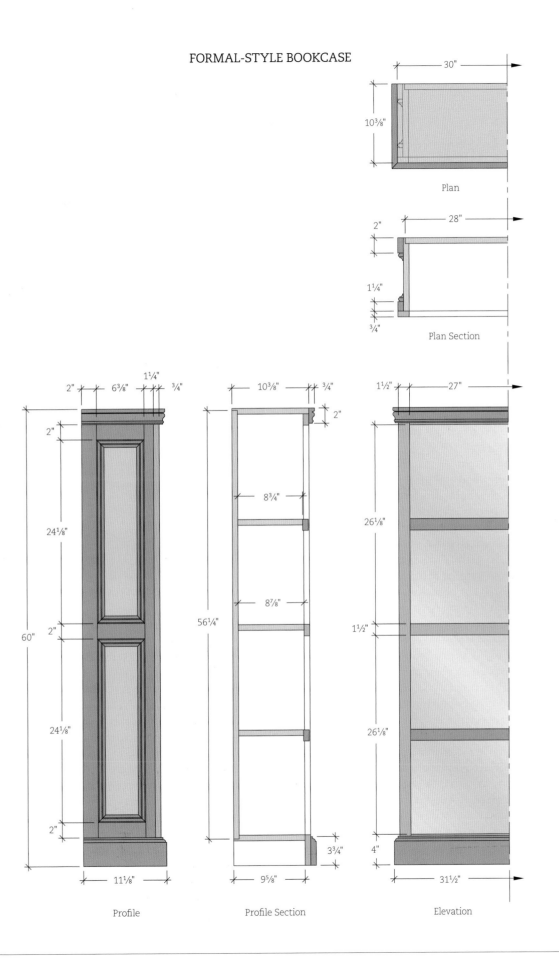

Plan

Plan Section

Profile

Profile Section

Elevation

CHAPTER TWO

The Science of Shelving

by Robert W. Lang

I t's always tempting to push things to their limits. How far can I drive with the needle on "E," how cold can the shop be and still have the glue dry, and how long can I make that shelf without it sagging? The answers to these questions might seem obvious, but in determining the size of shelves, many times the answers aren't simple. So we decided to take a look at the available scientific data, review our own experiences and perform some tests of our own.

In the end, we found that plywood can be tweaked to perform almost as well as solid wood – which surprised us. Here's how we reached this conclusion, which defies conventional wisdom.

The three most common materials used for shelves are solid wood, plywood and sheet materials such as particleboard and medium density fiberboard (MDF). While all of these are made from the same basic stuff, they have quite different structural characteristics. Knowing these characteristics, both the good and the bad, enables you to successfully make shelves that bear their loads without sagging or failing.

A lot of research has been done by the Forest Products Laboratory and by the Architectural Woodwork Institute, whose chart is reproduced at right. For those who enjoy physical science and crunching numbers, the "Wood Handbook" is available online at: fpl.fs.fed.us. This publication is a gold mine of data for most wood species and manufactured wood products. An online calculator, called "The Sagulator," also is available at woodbin.com/calcs/sagulator.htm.

For the rest of us, we can use the charts along with practical experience to set some reasonable limits, and find ways to produce good work that pushes the limits when we need to. We need to remember that like our children, every piece of wood is an individual, and each individual may not behave as we expect it to. We also need to keep in mind that the amount of deflection in a shelf will increase in time. This additional deflection can be as much as 50 percent of the original movement, so what you can get away with today may well prove to be unacceptable a year or so down the road.

Why Shelves Sag

Structurally, a piece of wood is a bundle of long fibers. These fibers have a tendency to bend and return to their original form. This is known as the "modulus of elasticity." They also have a tendency to stay rigid – known as the "modulus of rigidity." These factors have been established for most wood species, and can be plugged into different formulas to calculate how far a shelf of a given size will bend under a load.

Both of these tendencies are dependent on the length of the fibers, and the thickness and width of the bundle. Thicker and wider boards will have more fibers and therefore will be more resistant to bending under a load.

When the fibers increase in length the tendency to bend increases. This change is exponential – a relatively small increase in length will produce a large increase in the tendency to sag, and this is what gets us in trouble if we ignore it. As you can see from the chart at right, a 36"-long poplar shelf can support just a little more than half the weight that a 30" shelf can carry without sagging. Add another foot to the length and you're suddenly and unfortunately down to about a fourth of the original load.

With shelves, any increase in the number of long fibers present will increase the strength of the board. But keep in mind that you can't be entirely scientific when dealing with solid wood. Where and when the tree was grown and how the log was cut into boards can make a significant difference – even in boards of the same species. If the board is cut in a way that leaves much of the grain running off the edge, it won't be as strong as another.

Man-made boards, such as plywood, particleboard and MDF contain wood fibers in a different form, and are much more likely to sag under a load. Plywood has a slight advantage compared to other man-made boards because it still contains some long fibers in every other layer. Even so, a plywood shelf with no edge treatment will carry less than half the weight of a solid-wood shelf of the same length, and its performance is just a bit better than particleboard or MDF.

Particleboard and MDF have no continuous long fibers present, and have nearly no rigidity without some other means of support. MDF will carry roughly one-third of the load of solid wood, while particleboard will only support one-fourth of the load. Thicker parts will support more weight, but as length increases, the weight of these materials can lead to shelves that start to sag from their own weight.

Estimated Load in Pounds to Cause Shelf Deflection of ¼"

MATERIAL	THICKNESS	SPAN 30"		36"		42"		48"	
	WIDTH	8"	12"	8"	12"	8"	12"	8"	12"
Solid yellow poplar, red gum or sweet gum	¾"	322	483	189	284	117	175	78	117
	1⅟16"	912	1,368	528	790	332	498	221	332
Solid hard maple, pecan or red oak	¾"	356	534	209	313	133	206	88	133
	1⅟16"	1,021	1,536	592	888	373	560	249	374
Solid birch or hickory	¾"	400	600	232	348	146	219	98	146
	1⅟16"	1,134	1,701	660	990	414	621	277	415
Medium density particleboard (raw or covered with "melamine")	¾"	78	117	46	69	29	43	19	28
	1"	185	277	109	164	69	102	45	66
Medium density fiberboard (raw or covered with "melamine")	¾"	100	150	58	87	36	54	25	38
	1"	237	356	137	206	85	128	59	90
Birch faced plywood, veneer core	¾"	145	218	86	129	54	81	36	54
Birch faced plywood, medium density particleboard core	¾"	125	188	72	109	46	68	31	46
Medium density particleboard covered two sides and one edge with nominal 0.028" high pressure decorative laminate	¾" (core)	174	261	100	139	64	96	42	63
Medium density particleboard covered two sides and one edge with nominal 0.050" high pressure decorative laminate	¾" (core)	234	350	137	205	86	129	58	87
Medium density particleboard with ⅛" solid lumber edge	¾"	89	139	53	79	33	50	22	33
Medium density particleboard with ¾" solid lumber edge	¾"	100	150	60	90	42	63	25	38
Medium density particleboard with ¾" x 1½" solid lumber dropped edge	¾"	384	435	216	241	132	152	92	107

NOTE: All medium density particleboard is ANSI208.1-1998 Type M-2. The information and ratings stated here pertain to material currently offered and represent results of tests believed to be reliable. However, due to variations in handling and in methods not known or under our control, neither the AWI nor the AWMAC can make any warranties or guarantees as to end results.

Reprinted with permission from the 8th Edition Quality Standards Illustrated, Architectural Woodwork Institute, Reston, Va.

Key Design Aspects

The solution to making a strong shelf from plywood, particleboard or MDF is to add a solid-wood edge. In commonly used ¾"-thick pieces of sheet materials, the addition of a ¾" x 1½" solid-wood edge will yield a shelf with nearly the carrying capacity of solid wood. The width of the wood edge, in this case aligned vertically, provides support by lining up a lot of long fibers. The wider the edge, the more fibers will be present, yielding a stronger shelf.

This wood edge can be simply glued to the plywood or particleboard, but a shallow rabbet in the back of the solid-wood edge will make it easier to keep the pieces lined up. Biscuits or a tongue-and-groove joint can also be used as an aid to alignment.

My rule of thumb is to limit shelves that are made of man-made materials and do not have a solid-wood edge to shorter than 32", with an absolute maximum of 36". In addition to keeping the shelves within a safe working range, this keeps other parts of cabinets, such as doors and drawers, from becoming too wide. (Plus you can get a good yield from 4 x 8 sheets.)

At 36" wide I want to use at least a ¾" x ¾" piece of solid wood to reinforce the front edge. Anything longer than that, I use a wood edge at least ¾" thick by 1¼" wide. Of course, all of these "rules" must be considered in relation to what the shelves will carry.

With extreme lengths of shelves, or very heavy loads, a solid edge across the back of the shelf will add additional strength. A piece of ½"-square steel tubing screwed to the back of the solid edge and the bottom of the plywood shelf also helps.

For solid-wood shelves, the solution is to make a thicker shelf when long distances must be spanned. Increasing thickness to 1" from ¾" will add a lot of strength, and you can also add an edge to the front for even more support.

Our tests, as well as the research we studied, were conducted with shelves supported only on their ends. This represents a typical situation, as in an adjustable shelf in a cabinet, supported by pegs in holes. You also can gain strength if you physically add support to the back edge. With adjustable shelves this would be a row or two of holes and pegs that would hold up the back edge. If the shelf is permanently mounted in position, you can add a cleat for the back edge to rest on, or you can fasten through the back of the box and then into the edge of the shelf.

Some Surprising Test Results

Our testing was not entirely scientific; it would have taken a much larger sample and more precise measuring equipment than we had available, but our results do dramatically demonstrate what happens to commonly

Adding a ¾"-thick x 1½"-wide solid-wood edge to the plywood shelf gives it nearly the strength of the solid-wood shelf.

used materials under different loads and at different lengths. We tested five different materials, in lengths of 3', 4' and 5'.

We left out particleboard and MDF; we don't consider these materials suitable for quality woodwork. We tested solid red oak, solid poplar, maple plywood with a fir core, Baltic birch plywood and maple plywood with a solid-wood front edge.

All of our samples were ¾" thick and 9" wide. The maple plywood had nine plys, including the face veneers, and the Baltic birch plywood had 13 plys. The solid-wood front edge was a ¾"- x 1½"-piece of quartersawn ash. All of the material was selected at random; we went to our local supplier and picked wood from their available stock.

The results we obtained were generally in line with other available data, but there were a few surprises. We started our tests with 60"-long shelves, supported at each end, and applied weights and measured how far the shelf sagged. For each round of testing, we cut 12" off the end of each shelf and stacked on even more weight. To give you an idea of how this weight compares to your books at home, one lineal foot of 8½" x 11" books weighs about 35 pounds.

As shown on page 25, it's tough to make a workable shelf 5' long out of these materials. But the pictures do point out the difference in relative strength between plywood and solid wood. At this length, the plywood with the solid-wood edge (shown above) performed as well as the solid-wood shelf. This also points out one

5'-long Shelves Don't Hold Much Weight

MATERIAL	LENGTH	WEIGHT	SAG	WEIGHT	SAG
Solid oak	5'	50	¼"	150	⅝"
Solid poplar	5'	50	⅛"	150	⁷⁄₁₆"
Maple plywood	5'	50	½"	150	1⁷⁄₁₆"
Baltic birch plywood	5'	50	⁷⁄₁₆"	150	1¼"
Maple ply with solid edge	5'	50	⅛"	150	⁷⁄₁₆"

A 60"-long solid-wood shelf sags ⅝" under a load of 150 pounds. The flag in the photos indicates the position of the bottom of the shelf before any weight is applied.

A 60"-long plywood shelf sags three times as much under the same load. Our sample of maple plywood (shown here) sagged nearly 1½". Baltic birch plywood was a bit better, but it still sagged 1¼".

of the difficulties of trying to scientifically study wood. The poplar shelf performed slightly better than the oak, although all data and our expectation was that the oak would perform better. We still expect oak to be stronger; we think the difference was due to something about our poplar board. Had we tested a larger sample, the results would likely have been more in line with other tests.

A span of 4' is still wider than most of us would go, but there is quite a difference in the weight a shelf can carry. As shown in the chart and photos, the same weight will cause a sag that is only one-fourth to one-third of the amount in a longer shelf. Once again, the plywood shelf with a solid-wood edge (which is not shown in the photos above) performed nearly as well as the solid poplar and solid oak shelves.

At 3' all the shelves carried much larger loads before they began to sag. But what was a surprise was the performance of the plywood shelf with the solid edge. At longer lengths, it performed as well as the solid-wood sample. At 3', however, the solid shelves could now support extremely heavy weights without bending, but the plywood with the solid edge now performed more like the plywood shelves without an edge. So short plywood shelves might not be as strong as you think.

So what conclusions can we draw from all of this, and what advice can we give to woodworkers? A quick survey of our staff found that none of us would likely make a shelf more than 3' long unless we absolutely had to, regardless of material. If we had to go further than that, thicker solid wood, or plywood with solid-wood reinforcement, would be the logical choice.

When you design shelves, you need to consider practical matters as well as looks, and if the shelves are intended to carry something heavy, you may need to make some compromises. If you're tempted to push the limits the best thing to do is make a stronger shelf than you think you need. After all, the anvil has to be stored somewhere.

4'-long Shelves Show the Strength of Solid Wood

MATERIAL	LENGTH	WEIGHT	SAG	WEIGHT	SAG	WEIGHT	SAG
Solid oak	4'	50	0	150	3/16"	230	1/4"
Solid poplar	4'	50	0	150	1/8"	230	1/4"
Maple plywood	4'	50	1/8"	150	1/2"	230	7/8"
Baltic birch plywood	4'	50	3/16"	150	9/16"	230	3/4"
Maple ply with solid edge	4'	50	0	150	1/8"	230	1/4"

A 4'-long solid-wood poplar shelf bends much less than the 5'-long one, even though the weight has been increased to 230 pounds.

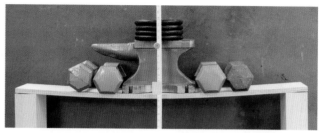

The difference in the amount of sag in maple plywood is also dramatic; it bends about half as much as the longer shelf with the increased weight.

3'-long Shelves in Solid Wood are Incredibly Strong

MATERIAL	LENGTH	WEIGHT	SAG	WEIGHT	SAG	WEIGHT	SAG	WEIGHT	SAG	WEIGHT	SAG
Solid oak	3'	50	0	100	0	150	0	230	1/16"	280	3/32"
Solid poplar	3'	50	0	100	0	150	0	230	0	280	1/16"
Maple plywood	3'	50	1/16"	100	1/8"	150	3/16"	230	1/4"	280	5/16"
Baltic birch plywood	3'	50	0	100	3/32"	150	1/8"	230	3/16"	280	1/4"
Maple ply with solid edge	3'	50	0	100	0	150	1/8"	230	3/16"	280	7/32"

At 3', which is about as long as our editors would go, the solid-wood poplar shelf will hold 150 pounds without deflecting. It only sags a minimal amount at the maximum weight we tested – 230 pounds (shown here).

While the performance of the maple plywood shelf is better at this shorter length, there is still 1/8" of sag at 150 pounds and 1/4" of sag at 280 pounds (shown here). Adding a solid-wood edge would help – a little.

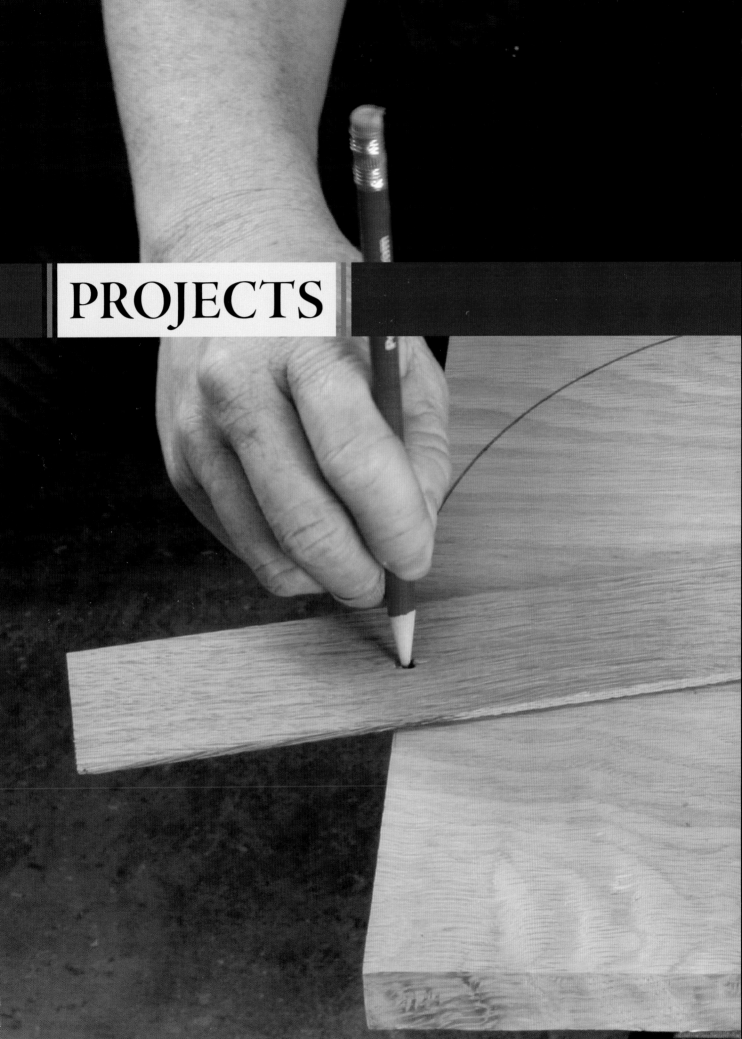

PROJECTS

CHAPTER THREE

Four-hour Bookcase

by David Thiel

Sometimes you need more storage space, pure and simple. This 6'-tall bookcase is well within your grasp using the simple techniques outlined here.

Don't snicker at the promises at the top of this page. We went to our local home-center store and purchased five 1 x 10 x 6' and one 1 x 3 x 8' dimensional pine boards, 28 square feet of ⁵⁄₁₆"-thick tongue-and-groove beadboard paneling and an 8' length of crown moulding. Total cost: $115. By purchasing the lumber already dimensioned to ¾" thickness, we saved lots of time, and avoided the need for a planer and jointer.

I used a table saw to cut the lumber to width and length, a router (with just one bit and one setup) to cut

the joints, a miter saw to cut the moulding, a random-orbit sander, a couple clamps, a hammer, nail set and a drill. That's all you need in your shop to make this (or a whole library) of sturdy and attractive bookcases.

If this were garage shelving, you could have screwed the fixed shelves in place and walked away. But we wanted these shelves to have the strength of traditional cabinetry. These same techniques can also be used to produce oak, walnut or cherry shelving if that's your preference, but the cost will be greater.

To support and align the three fixed shelves we plowed ¼"-deep x ¾"-wide dados in both side pieces. The top dado is located 1⅜" down from the top edge.

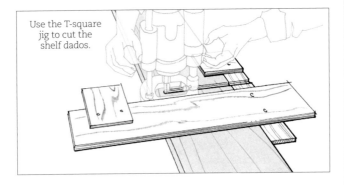

Use the T-square jig to cut the shelf dados.

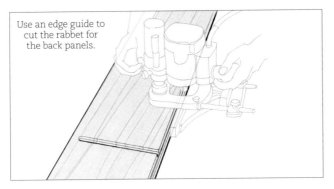

Use an edge guide to cut the rabbet for the back panels.

This locates the cabinet's fixed top (called out as a fixed shelf in the cutting list) so the bottom edge of the crown moulding will overlay the shelf by ⅜" (this allows room for nailing the crown in place). The bottom dado is cut 2¼" up from the bottom to allow a 2¼"-wide kick strip. The middle fixed shelf and dado are centered between the upper and lower fixed shelves.

With these dados created I used the same router setup (a ¾"-diameter straight bit making a ¼"-deep cut) to run a rabbet on the back edge of both of the sides. Like many quality routers, the DeWalt DW621 plunge router comes with an edge guide that allows us to set the ¾" bit to take only a ⅜"-wide pass while guiding along the back edge of the side.

With the joinery complete, the rest is easy. Glue is not adequate to hold everything together, so we opted to

Cutting List

NO.	PART	SIZES (INCHES)			MATERIAL	NOTES
		T	W	L		
2	Sides	¾"	9¼"	72"	Pine	
3	Fixed shelves	¾"	8⅞"	29"	Pine	
3	Adjustable shelves	¾"	8½"	28½"	Pine	
1	Kick	¾"	2½"	28½"	Pine	
1	Hanging strip	¾"	2½"	28½"	Pine	
1	Back	5⁄16"	29"	68"	Pine	Paneling
1	Crown moulding	9⁄16"	2¼"	60"	Pine	

Toenailing

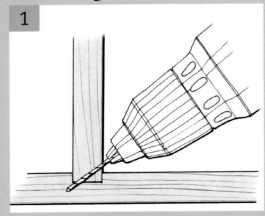

1

Set the length of the bit to be slightly shorter than the length of the nail.

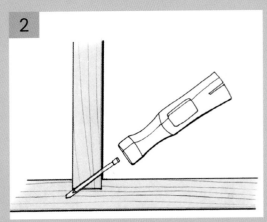

2

Sink the nail until the hammer's head is almost to the wood.

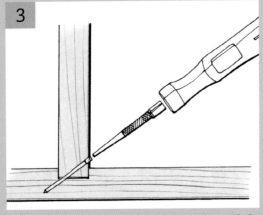

3

Make sure you use a nail set that has a tip sized properly for the nail you're using.

One trick I use when nailing is to prepare the face of the hammer head by roughing it up with sandpaper. This keeps the face from slipping off the nail set (or nail head) when struck.

use an old woodworking technique that isn't discussed enough these days: toenailing.

Toenailing is the process of angling a nail through one board and into another board to lock the two boards together. This is done from inside a corner to hide the nail, while still providing strength. A hammer and nail set (which is a steel rod used to drive a nail under the surface of wood) are the low-priced tools for this technique.

Toenailing is a three-step process. After gluing and clamping the joint (hold the shelf with the back edge flush to the rabbet) drill a pilot hole with a bit slightly smaller in diameter than the brad or finish nail being used.

With the pilot hole drilled, slowly tap the nail in. Because you're hammering into a corner you must stop short of putting the nail all the way in. The hammer head can't reach into the corner – try it and you'll make a real mess of that soft pine. Use a nail set to drive the nail home. I recommend three nails per joint.

With all the nails set, add the kick (set it ¾" back from the front edge of the lower shelf) and the hanging strip (flush to the inside edge of the cabinet's top) using glue, clamps and a couple of nails through the sides.

The back is tongue-and-groove paneling (purchased ready-to-use in 8' lengths) cut to size and nailed in place. Use one nail (centered on each back board) in the top, middle and bottom fixed shelves to hold the back in place.

Now cut, fit, glue and nail the crown moulding in place to the case's top and sides. Putty your nail holes and any gaps. The loose shelves simply rest on some shelf pins.

The last decision is how to finish the case. I was lucky enough to find some clear (no knots or sap) pine that will take a nice clear coat of lacquer or a wipe-on oil finish. But you could certainly add a coat of paint to finish things up as well.

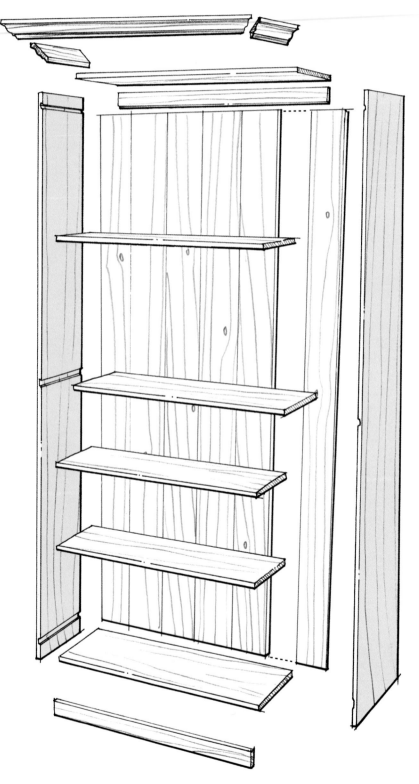

Exploded View

CHAPTER FOUR

Shaker Shelves

by Megan Fitzpatrick

With this project we'll teach you a few clever tricks to draw arcs without a compass, and to straighten twisted boards – which is often a problem when working with wider pieces of wood.

This modified Shaker design, downsized from a set of creamery shelves, is adapted from a Shaker Workshops catalog. To ensure our ¾"-stock would not bow under the weight of even the heaviest items, we decided to make these shelf pieces a bit shorter than those you'll find on the company's web site (shakerworkshops.com).

Many home centers carry only pine, poplar and oak (you may also find maple or aspen, depending on your region). We decided on oak because we think it has the best natural appearance.

One of the biggest challenges you'll have with this project is finding wide boards that are straight and flat … and that remain straight and flat after you cut them to size. Take time to look through the racks for the best boards – and if at all possible, avoid shrink-wrapped boards, no matter how pretty. You'll need two 6' and one

A thin piece of scrap, a nail and a drill are all it takes to make this simple compass jig.

Because the wood for the sides and shelves is 11¼"-wide and your miter saw is likely a 10" model, you'll have to cut the pieces in two steps. Measure and make the first cut. Then flip the board over and line up the saw blade to the kerf you've already cut, and make the second cut.

4' 1 x 12s (or one 10' and one 8' length). You'll also need a 6' length of 1 x 4 for the supports.

Once you're back in the shop, your first step is to cut the sides to length on your miter saw. If you have a 10" miter saw, your crosscuts on the sides (and shelves) will be a two-step process because the diameter of the saw blade limits the width of the cut. You'll need to first cut on one side of your board, then flip it over and carefully line up the kerf with the saw blade before completing the cut (see picture above).

Now, you're ready to lay out the arched top and cutout at the bottom. Align the top edges of the sides and stick the faces together with double-stick tape to keep them from slipping, then clamp both pieces together flat to your workbench. Now, measure across the width to find the center of your board, and make a mark. That measurement is the same distance you'll measure down from the top edge to mark the intersection of the two points (5⅝"unless you've resized the plan, or used different-sized stock). This point is where you'll place your compass point to draw the half-circle arch across the top.

And if you don't have a compass, it's no problem. It's easy to make a compass jig. Simply grab a thin piece of scrap and drive a nail through the middle near one end. Now, using the same measurement you already established to find the compass point (again, it's 5⅝" on our plan), mark and drill a hole that distance from the nail, and stick a pencil point through it. Voilà – a compass jig.

You can use that same jig for the bottom arched cutout. Simply drill another hole 3⅛" away from your nail. Set the nail as close to the center of the bottom edge as possible and mark the cutout arch. Or, mark the arch with a traditional compass.

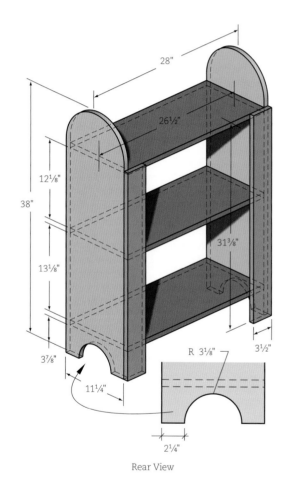

Rear View

Cutting List

NO.	ITEM	DIMENSIONS (INCHES)			MATERIAL
		T	W	L	
2	Sides	¾"	11¼"	38"	Oak
3	Shelves	¾"	11¼"	26½"	Oak
2	Supports	¾"	3½"	31⅜"	Oak

Make sure your drill is at a 90° angle to the most narrow stock through which you're drilling – in this case, the ¾" edge of the side beneath the support.

You can pull a cup out of a board by clamping the piece to a straight-edge and pulling it tight with clamps before screwing it down.

Now use your jigsaw to cut as close to the lines as possible, and use a rasp and sandpaper to clean up the cuts. If you keep the pieces clamped together during this process, you should end up with nearly identical arches. If you're not confident in your jigsaw skills, practice making curved cuts on some scrap pieces before moving on to the real thing.

Now cut the shelves to length.

Set up your pocket-hole jig for ¾"-thick material. Mark the placement for three pocket holes on each end of each shelf, two of them ¾" from each long edge, and one in the center of the end. Drill the holes.

Cut the back supports to length, and sand all pieces to #150-grit before assembly (#120 if you're planning to paint).

Now you're ready for assembly, and the second trick we promised. Lay one side flat on your bench and mark the location of the top shelf at either side. You may not be able to line up the shelf with your marks because of cupping in the wide board; that's where the trick comes in. Position the back support (or any straight piece of scrap) along the bowed side of the shelf, if there is one,

and use clamps to bring the edges of the shelf flat to the support or straight scrap. Slide the clamped unit to the layout lines, hold or clamp it in place then use screws to attach. This trick will work to pull the bow from any of the shelves.

Attach all three shelves to both sides, straightening the pieces where necessary.

Now lay the assembly face down, line up the support with the top of your top shelf. Drill countersunk holes at the top shelf, at the bottom shelf, and at the inside edge where the support meets the middle shelf. Be sure to hold your drill at 90° to the sides; because you're drilling into ¾" stock, you could easily drill through the side if you're not careful.

Attach the uprights with #8 x 1¼" screws (rubbing the threads on some wax will help them seat more easily). Pay particular attention at the top and bottom as the stock can easily split. If it does crack, stop your drill immediately – but don't panic. Just back the screw out a tiny bit, and the split will close up.

Finish the shelves with two coats of wiping varnish.

CHAPTER FIVE

Craftsman Bookcase

by Robert W. Lang

There are many bookcases in my house, but they're a motley collection – poor cousins to the rest of the furniture. The really nice bookcases I've made have gone to live with clients, while I have kept the prototypes and the also-rans. They are nicer than concrete blocks and pine planks, but not my best work. The cherry bookcase in my living room was a test case – both of a dovetail jig and the wood's moisture content.

It was time for something nicer. This design is an adaptation of early 20th-century Gustav Stickley bookcases. I wanted to use nice wood, and show off a bit with the joinery.

I didn't have a specific species of wood in mind when I went to the lumberyard, but I knew I wanted something attractive and wide enough to avoid gluing up individual boards. I found a nice batch of sapele, also known as African mahogany, and brought home 50 board feet of wide planks.

Off to a Good Start

My lumber had been surfaced to $^{15}/_{16}$", but it wasn't quite flat. After cutting the parts to rough sizes, I ran the material over the jointer and through the planer to remedy that, ending up with stock slightly thicker than

This dado jig is made to fit the thickness of the shelves, and utilizes a flush-cutting bit with the bearing on top.

$^{13}/_{16}$". I planed off the mill marks with a smoothing plane, and dressed all of the stock with a scraper before working on the joinery.

This exercise served two purposes: I now knew the material was straight and true, and having the faces at a nearly finished state would save work later on. It's a lot easier to work on a plank on a bench than it is to work inside an assembled cabinet.

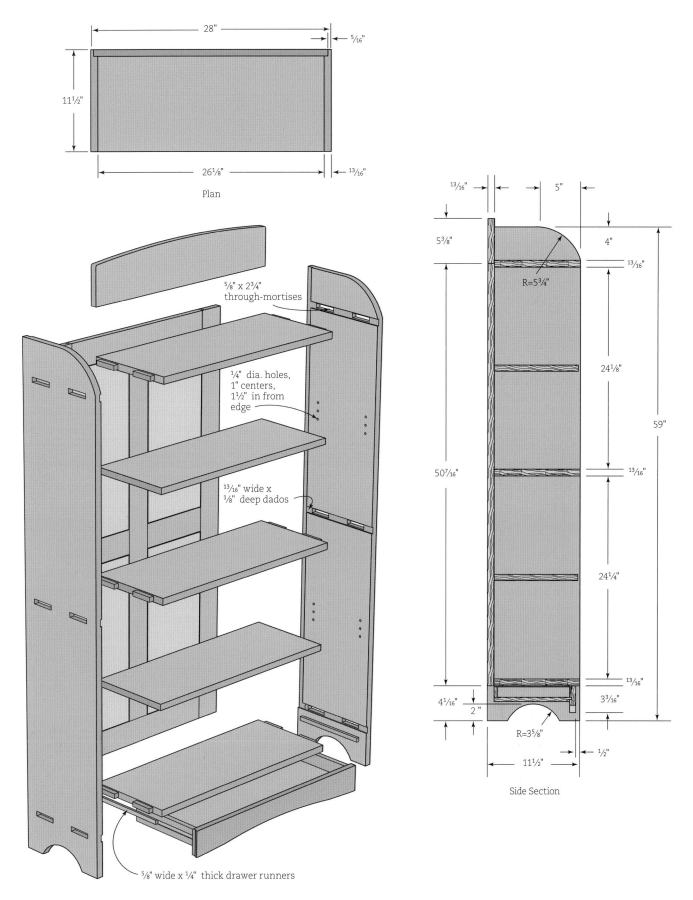

28"

5/16"

11½"

26⅛"

13/16"

Plan

⅝" x 2¾"
through-mortises

¼" dia. holes,
1" centers,
1½" in from
edge

13/16" wide x
⅛" deep dados

⅝" wide x ¼" thick drawer runners

Exploded View

13/16"

5"

5⅜"

4"

R=5¾"

13/16"

24⅛"

59"

50 7/16"

13/16"

24¼"

13/16"

4 1/16"

3 3/16"

2 "

R=3⅝"

½"

11½"

Side Section

When the faces were smooth, I cut the sides and fixed shelves to their final sizes. I determined which side should be right and which should be left, situating the most attractive faces on the outside. I put a 1"-diameter straight bit in my plunge router, and set the fence to cut a ⅞"-wide, ½"-deep rabbet on the back edge of each side, stopping at the bottom edge of the lowest shelf.

Doing this step first established the sides as right and left, and it kept me from confusing the inside and outside faces as I worked on the remaining joints. Each of the three shelves connects to the cabinet sides with a pair of wedged through-tenons. On the inside of the case, each shelf sits in a ⅛"-deep dado.

The dados aren't really needed structurally, but they ensure that the inner surfaces of the joints always look good, and they help to locate the through-mortises with the jigs that I used. With a dozen through-mortises to fit, I needed a method to make the process efficient and idiot-resistant, if not idiot-proof.

Jigs and Joints Work Together

Because I didn't have a router bit the exact size to match the thickness of the shelves, I decided to use a ⅝"-diameter, ½"-long bit with a guide bearing mounted above the cutters. I made a jig to match the thickness of the shelves by clamping an offcut from one of the shelves between the two fences.

I then screwed a straight piece of scrap to one end of the fences, making certain that the inner edge was square to the working edges of the fences. I screwed another piece of scrap to the opposite end of the fences, and I was ready to make a test cut. The resulting dado was just a bit narrow, and a few swipes with the smoothing plane on the bottom of the shelves made for a snug fit.

After routing the three dados in each of the case sides, I began to make the second jig, which is used to cut the mortises. The mortises are ⅝" wide and 2¾" long, and they are equal distances from the front and back of the case sides with a 3" space in between. Rather than cut the mortises in the jig, I made them by assembling pieces of ½"-thick plywood in two layers.

I laid out the locations of the mortises on the larger, bottom part of the jig, then I glued and nailed smaller pieces along the layout lines. I drilled holes in the waste area, and with a flush-trim bit in my router, I trimmed the bottom of the jig to match the top. A few cuts with a chisel to clean out the corners and I was ready to make mortises – almost.

The mortises need to be exactly centered in the dados, and I needed a way for the jig to be clamped to the case sides. I made an edge piece the thickness of the case side, plus the thickness of the jig, and used the same jig that I used to cut the dados in the sides to cut a notch across this piece. This notch aligns the jig to the shelf dados.

After carefully centering this piece on the mortises, I screwed it in place and made a test cut. I used an offcut from one of the shelves to align the jig for routing. I jammed the offcut in the dado in the case side, leaving an inch or so protruding from the edge of the side. This allowed me to knock the notch in the jig over the scrap. With the jig properly aligned to the case side, I clamped it in place. After drilling a hole to get the bit started, I cut the mortises with a flush-trim bit in my router.

After routing each pair of mortises, I left the jig clamped in place, flipped the side over and used the jig as a guide to cut the corners of the mortises square with a chisel.

At this point, I walked away from mortise-and-tenon territory and went to work on the curved profiles at the top front corner of each side, and the arched cutouts at the bottom. After laying out the curves on one side, I cut close to the line with a jigsaw and cleaned up the edges with a rasp.

The first side was put into service as a template for the second. I put the finished side on top of the other and traced the curves. After cutting the curves in the second side, I clamped the two together, and used a flush-cutting bit in the router to make the second side an exact match of the first.

Cutting List

NO.	ITEM	DIMENSIONS (INCHES)			MATERIAL	COMMENTS
		T	W	L		
2	Sides	13⁄16"	11½"	59"	Sapele	
3	Fixed shelves	13⁄16"	10 11⁄16"	28⅛"	Sapele	
2	Adjustable shelves	13⁄16"	10 7⁄16"	26¼"	Sapele	
2	Back panel outer stiles	13⁄16"	3 5⁄16"	50 7⁄16"	Sapele	
1	Back panel inner stile	13⁄16"	3"	46 5⁄16"	Sapele	1¼" TBE *
1	Back panel top rail	13⁄16"	3"	23¼"	Sapele	1¼" TBE *
1	Back panel bottom rail	13⁄16"	3⅝"	23¼"	Sapele	1¼" TBE *
2	Back panel middle rails	13⁄16"	3"	11⅜"	Sapele	1¼" TBE *
4	Back panels	¾"	9⅝"	21⅛"	Sapele	
1	Back splash	13⁄16"	5⅜"	27½"	Sapele	
1	Lower apron/ drawer front	13⁄16"	3 3⁄16"	26⅜"	Sapele	
2	Drawer sides	⅝"	1¾"	10 1⁄16"	Maple	
1	Drawer back	½"	1¼"	26⅛"	Maple	
1	Drawer bottom	½"	9¾"	25⅜"	Poplar	
2	Drawer runners	⅜"	¾"	9 1⁄16"	Maple	

* TBE=Tenon both ends

This jig for the through-mortises is made by assembling small pieces to a backer. The openings are then cut with a router and a locating fence is added.

After routing, the mortising jig also serves as a guide for the chisel to square the corners of the through-mortises.

A Trip to Through-Tenon Territory

The next step is where the dados in the case sides saved a tremendous amount of time and prevented the formation of even more grey hair. The layout for the tenons needs to match the mortise locations exactly.

At this point I looked at the three shelves, marked the best face and edge of each, and decided which one would be the top, middle and bottom. I clamped the entire cabinet together and with a lumber crayon, marked the locations of the shelves in relation to the cabinet sides.

Some hand fitting would be needed, and putting a carefully fit bottom shelf upside down in the top shelf location wouldn't be a good thing. With the case together, I ran the point of my knife around the perimeter of each mortise, marking the location of the tenons in the ends of the shelves.

I set up a small plunge router with a fence set to leave the tenons slightly proud of the outside of the cabinet

After cutting the lower arch with a jigsaw, the curve is smoothed with a rasp.

After the curves on one side are completed, the first side is used as a template to make the second side.

With a soft pencil, I made a series of hatch marks on the tenon cheeks and eased them into place. When I met resistance, I removed the shelf and examined the marks. The tight spots showed as smears in the pencil lines and I used a float to reduce the thickness until I had a good fit.

A Further Complication

Clearly in the grips of an obsessive-compulsive exposed-joinery episode, I laid out each tenon end for a pair of wedges. Unable to leave well enough alone, I decided it would look nice to set the wedges on a slight angle, making dovetail-like shapes in the end of each tenon.

I marked the distance to the edge of each cut on the ends of the tenons with a combination square, then marked the angles with a bevel gauge and knife. The slots for the wedges are at a compound angle, but I only fussed about the start of each cut. Using a dovetail saw, I cut the vertical angles by eye.

This meant that the wedges also had to be a complex shape. I began by cutting simple wedges from a piece of purpleheart, about 1" thick, 8" wide and 1½" long. I set the miter gauge on the band saw to 3° and made the wedges by making a cut, flipping the wood over and making a second cut.

I put each wedge in place, trimmed off the end with a saw, then pared the edges with a chisel to match the tenon cheeks. To keep the wedges organized, after fitting a group I stuck them in order on a strip of blue painter's tape, then stuck the tape to the face of each shelf. On final assembly, each group of wedges would be where they belonged.

sides. I set the depth to the top of the knife marks, checking both sides of each end to be sure that the tenons were centered. I wanted to make the cheek cuts quickly, but I didn't want to go too far.

I cut the edge cheeks of the tenons with a dovetail saw, and used a jigsaw to remove the waste between the two tenons. With the end of each shelf housed in the dado these cuts didn't need to be pretty; I only needed to get material out of the way.

Before starting the fitting process, I took a chisel and chamfered the inside edge of each mortise, and with a piece of sandpaper I broke the sharp edge of each tenon to prevent damage to the outside of the mortises during fitting.

The tenons are marked directly from the mortises, ensuring that the locations match.

A shallow rabbet is cut on each side of the shelves to start the making of the tenons.

The ends of the tenons are cut by hand, then the waste in between is removed.

Penciled hatch marks on the tenons will smear to reveal tight spots within the joints during test fitting.

The pencil lines smear where material needs to be removed. A planemaker's float gives good control and leaves a smooth surface.

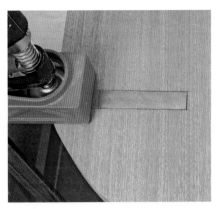

The ends can be a bit loose because the wedges will expand the tenons.

In theory, the tapered wedges will fit anywhere. In reality, I fit each one and kept them in order.

Each wedge is pared flush with the surrounding tenon. Then they are removed and stuck to a piece of blue painter's tape

For assembly, I used liquid hide glue to allow plenty of open time to put the joints together and set the wedges in place. After clamping the assembly, I brushed glue in each slot then drove the wedges in with a hammer. While the glue was drying, I made the back panel.

This panel is straightforward: The rails and stiles join with mortises and tenons that are haunched at the top and bottom extremes to fill the grooves for the panels. The panels are slightly thinner than the frame, and they are raised on both sides. The panel was made about 1/16" too wide to allow for fitting to the case, and the top is trimmed to land in the center of the top shelf.

Back to Level Ground

When the glue on the case had completely dried, it was time to trim the wedges and exposed tenons down to the surface of the case sides. The first step was to use a flush-cutting saw to remove the ends of the wedges. Then I

took a rag soaked with mineral spirits, and wet the ends of the tenons.

This saturation makes the tough end-grain fibers easier to trim with a block plane. The final bit of leveling was with a card scraper and when the tenons were flush, I scraped the entire surface of both cabinet sides.

I had set aside a small piece of stock for the backsplash. The grain on this piece arched to match the profile I intended to cut, and with the back in place in the carcase, I trimmed it to final width and length, then marked the curved top edge. After cutting the shape on the band saw, I removed the saw marks with my block plane and shaped the corners with a rasp where the splash meets the case sides.

I've Got a Secret

The arched apron below the lowest shelf also was selected with the curve of the grain centered on the

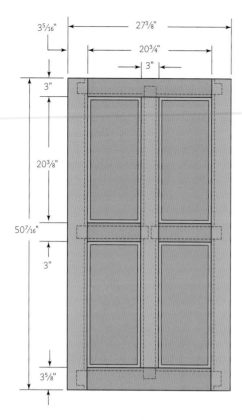

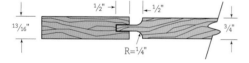

Back Panel

cut-out shape. The apron attaches to the cabinet in an unusual way. It actually is the front of a hidden drawer.

The apron is $1/16$" shorter than the distance between the two sides of the cabinet, and the $5/8$"-thick maple drawer sides are $1\frac{3}{4}$" wide and $10\frac{1}{4}$" long. The sides join the drawer front with half-blind dovetails, and are set in from the ends about $1/8$" on each side. A $3/4$"-wide, $1/8$"-deep groove was cut in the outer face of each drawer side after the drawer was assembled to hang the drawer on runners.

The drawer runners are strips of maple, $3/4$" wide x $1/4$" thick, held to the cabinet sides with screws. The reason for setting the drawer sides in was to leave the smallest possible gap between the ends of the drawer front and the cabinet sides, and to make the runners a substantial thickness.

A small rabbeted lip is left on the end grain of the drawer front, so that any trimming needed to fit the front would be on this small edge. I'd seen a similar detail on an original drawer, and was curious to see if it would be as easy to trim and fit as it first appeared. The final fitting was indeed easier, but this complicated the drawer construction.

I cut the dovetail joints at the front and made the sockets between the pins $1/8$" deeper than the thickness of the drawer sides. After fitting the pieces, I took them apart, and cut the rabbets on the ends of the drawer front at the table saw. When I was satisfied with the joints at the front of the drawer, I cut the drawer back to length, then cut the through-dovetails at the rear of the drawer's sides.

Setting the sides of the drawer in from the ends of the drawer front posed a problem for letting in the groove for the drawer runners. I used a small router with a fence to cut the grooves, but had to temporarily attach

After sawing off the wedges, the joints are soaked with paint thinner to make it easier to trim the end grain flush.

Following the plane, a scraper is used to smooth the exposed tenon ends and the cabinet sides.

Located below the shelf and ½" back from the front edge, the drawer appears to be a fixed apron.

The rabbet in the end of the drawer front provides clearance for the sides, while allowing a narrow margin to be trimmed easily.

thin pieces of scrap on each side of the groove location to keep the base of the router above the end of the drawer front's lip.

After cutting the grooves, I carefully measured back 1" from the inside edge of the rabbet on each side. The fence on the router left the grooves short of this, so I used a chisel to extend the groove to this line, squaring up the end of the groove in the process. It's important that the grooves end at the same point, so that the ends of the runners can act as drawer stops.

I cut the maple runners and fit them to the width of the grooves in the drawer sides. Gravity will keep the top edge of the groove in contact with the runner, so the runner can be sized to slide easily. I left a margin of ⅟₃₂" so that the drawer won't bind if the runner swells in width.

After fitting the width, I planed the faces of the runners until the combined width of the drawer and runners with both runners in place was ¹⁄₁₆" less than the inside of the cabinet. There needs to be some room to allow for easy movement of the drawer, but not so much as to make the drawer sloppy.

The drawer bottom is ½" thick, and slides into ¼"-wide, ¼"-deep grooves in the insides of the drawer sides and front. I used the same setup on the router table for raising the back panels to form the tongue on three edges of the drawer bottom. The back of the drawer is ½" narrower than the sides to allow the bottom to slide in after the drawer is assembled. A couple screws in elongated holes secure the thick back edge of the bottom to the drawer back and allow for seasonal wood movement.

With the drawer completely assembled, I measured in from the front of the case 2⁵⁄₁₆" (the ¹³⁄₁₆" thickness of the drawer front, plus the 1" distance from the back of the front to the end of the groove in

the side, plus the ½" set-back of the drawer front from the front of the case).

I measured down from the bottom of the lowest shelf and drew a line parallel to the shelf to locate the runner. With the drawer front ½" behind the edge of the shelf, the top of the drawer front can't be seen when it is closed, so I left a ¹⁄₁₆" gap so the drawer wouldn't scrape the shelf on its way in and out. When I had the positions of the runners located, I screwed them to the inside of the case with #6 x ⅝" flathead screws.

Easy Elbow Grease Finish

Because I had planed and scraped all the large flat surfaces before assembly, there wasn't much to be done to get ready for finishing the bookcase. I planed the front edges of the fixed shelves flush to the cabinet sides, chamfered all of the edges slightly with a block plane, and gave everything a light sanding with #240-grit.

The first coat of finish was Watco Light Walnut Danish Oil. I saturated the surface, wet-sanded it with a nylon abrasive pad, kept the surface wet for about 45 minutes, then wiped off the excess. This was followed by two coats a day of Waterlox for three days. After allowing the finish to cure for a couple days, I wet-sanded it with Watco Satin Wax and #400-grit wet/dry paper, leaving a nice sheen and a surface that is pleasant to the touch.

The joinery, details and finish on this bookcase are more than what is needed to store some books, but that really wasn't the purpose in making it. The idea was to leave something behind that demonstrates what a bit of extra effort looks like. It makes me look like a competent craftsman. Now to fill it with some books that might make me look intelligent, as well.

The hidden drawer rides on wooden slides attached to the carcase. The end of the groove will act as a stop for the runners, and needs to end in the right spot.

The drawer bottom slides past the drawer back and into grooves in the sides and front. Screws in elongated holes will hold the bottom to the back and allow the bottom to shrink or swell.

Maple runners below the bottom shelf support and guide the hidden drawer.

CHAPTER SIX

Gustav Stickley's No. 72 Magazine Cabinet

by Christopher Schwarz

If you had been shopping for a magazine cabinet in 1910 and came across this piece in Gustav Stickley's catalog, chances are you would have turned the page with barely a glance.

The photo of the No. 72 Magazine Cabinet in the 1910 catalog is horrible. Someone in Gustav Stickley's art department mangled the picture, and it bears almost no resemblance to the real thing. The legs look both spindly and lumpy. The shelves don't look sturdy at all.

In real life, this piece of furniture is impressive. It was one of several pieces of furniture designed by Harvey Ellis, an architect, painter and designer. Ellis's short stint with Gustav Stickley's company before Ellis' death in 1904 was remarkably fruitful. Under his talented pen, a fair number of Stickley's massive and overbuilt furniture forms became lighter and a bit more graceful.

The No. 72 Magazine Cabinet is a good example of this period. The curved top rails and tapered legs all conspire to make this piece look more delicate than it is.

Like most Arts & Crafts projects, this one is straightforward to build. I used about 15 board feet of 4/4 mahogany, four board feet of 5/4, and six board feet of 8/4 – I had a little wood left over, but that always beats a second trip to the lumberyard. The plans for this project were developed by Robert W. Lang for his book "More Shop Drawings for Craftsman Furniture" (Cambium Press).

Start with the Sides

Most of the work on this project is in the two assemblies that make up the sides of the cabinet. And the heart of these side assemblies is the side panels.

These two panels have a tongue on the two long edges that are glued into a groove in the legs. Dados in the panels hold the shelves in place. And the rails are tenoned into mortises in the legs. Finally, the top is screwed down to the cabinet using cleats.

The first task is to prepare the side panels to be glued between the legs. I used a traditional tongue-and-groove joint. It's more elaborate than simply gluing the panel between the legs without joinery. However, it also guarantees you will have no visible gap between the legs and panel.

There are a variety of ways to cut the groove in the legs: A router table and a plow plane come to mind. I prefer to use a straight bit in a router with an edge guide. This allows me to see my cut at all times.

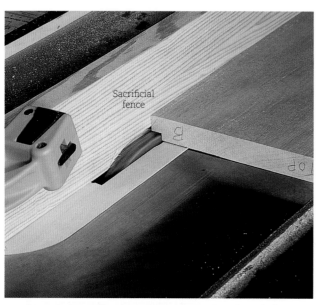

Sacrificial fence

Cut the tongues on the edges of the side panels using a dado stack in your table saw (plus a sacrificial fence). You also could use a rabbeting bit in your router table.

When your grooves and tongues are complete, they should fit snugly as shown. If you're not up to this task, you could simply glue the panel to the legs without any joinery. Just make sure you keep everything lined up so you're certain you'll achieve a tight joint.

Who Was Harvey Ellis?

Though Harvey Ellis worked for Gustav Stickley for only about a year until he died in 1904, Ellis's work left an indelible impression on Stickley's furniture. Chunky forms became lighter. Rails became curved. Legs became tapered on the sides. And – perhaps most significantly – some furniture became inlaid.

Before Ellis's stint with Stickley, Ellis led an itinerant life as an avant-garde painter, graphic designer, draftsman and sometimes architect, according to scholars. Born in Rochester, N.Y., in 1852, Ellis displayed an early knack for art as a child. His father decided he needed more discipline and sent him to West Point in 1871, according to the Harvey Ellis papers at the University of Rochester. Ellis was discharged from the military school for "tardiness, personal untidiness and gross neglect in his French assignments," according to the papers. There also were rumors of an affair with an actress.

Ellis went to New York to study art at the National Academy of Design, but he ended up as an architectural draftsman for Arthur Gilman instead. He returned to Rochester in 1877 and set up an architectural office with his brother, and together they designed many public buildings. After seven years or so Ellis left the firm and designed houses and public structures for cities across the Midwest. He rejoined his brother's firm in 1894 and also started designing interiors and becoming interested in the Arts & Crafts movement.

After separating from his wife, Ellis joined the staff of Stickley's magazine, *The Craftsman*, and began designing furniture and writing stories for the influential publication. He died in January 1904 at the age of 52, in part due to acute alcoholism, according to the university papers.

If you want to do things in this more traditional way, begin by milling a ½"-wide, ⅜"-deep and 31¾"-long stopped groove on the leg in the location shown in the diagram. Square out the groove where it stops using a chisel.

Now cut a matching tongue on the two long edges of your panel. You want the fit to be as near perfect as possible.

To keep things neat, I used a backsaw to cut a small shoulder on the bottom corners of the panel that conceals where the groove ends.

Before you can glue the side panel between the legs, you need to cut the ¼"-deep by ¾"-wide dados that hold the shelves. Use the diagrams on page 45 to lay out the

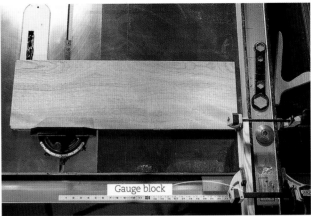

Cut the dados in the side panels using this setup on your table saw or a straight edge and a hand-held router. The gauge block on the right of the blade keeps the panel from getting caught between the fence and the blade.

You'll need to notch the bottom of the side panel to fit in the leg groove. A backsaw makes quick work of this simple operation (above). Clean up the cut with a sharp chisel and you're ready to move on (right).

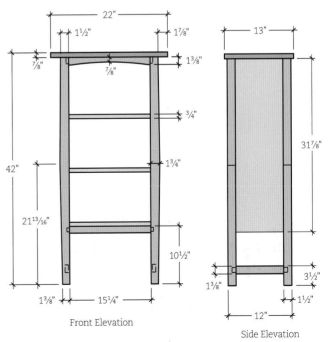

Front Elevation

Side Elevation

locations of the dados, then cut them using your dado stack as shown in the photo.

If all this seems complicated, the sides can be simplified. Make your side panels 9" wide instead of 9¾" and don't cut the tongues and grooves. Cut the dados for the shelves and then simply glue the panels between the legs.

The long-grain joint between the side panel and legs is stronger than the wood itself – you'll just have to be careful about lining everything up and making sure your stock is milled perfectly to avoid any gaps between the legs and the side panels.

Before you glue anything up, however, you're going to want to first cut the mortises in the legs. So set your parts aside and fit the shelves in their dados.

To prevent tearout where the dado stack exits the side panel, put down a couple pieces of masking tape to support the wood fibers. This really works.

Cutting List

NO.	ITEM	DIMENSIONS (INCHES)			MATERIAL	COMMENTS
		T	W	L		
4	Legs	1½"	1¾"	41⅛"	Mahogany	
2	Side stretchers	⅝"	1⅜"	10½"	Mahogany	¾" TBE
2	Side panels	¾"	9¾"	31⅞"	Mahogany	⅜" tongue, 2 edges
2	Bottom rails	¾"	1¼"	16¾"	Mahogany	¾" TBE
2	Arched top rails	¾"	1⅜"	16¾"	Mahogany	¾" TBE
3	Shelves	¾"	11¾"	15¾"	Mahogany	
1	Top	⅞"	13"	22"	Mahogany	
2	Cleats	½"	½"	8"	Mahogany	Attach top to sides

KEY: TBE = tenon on both ends

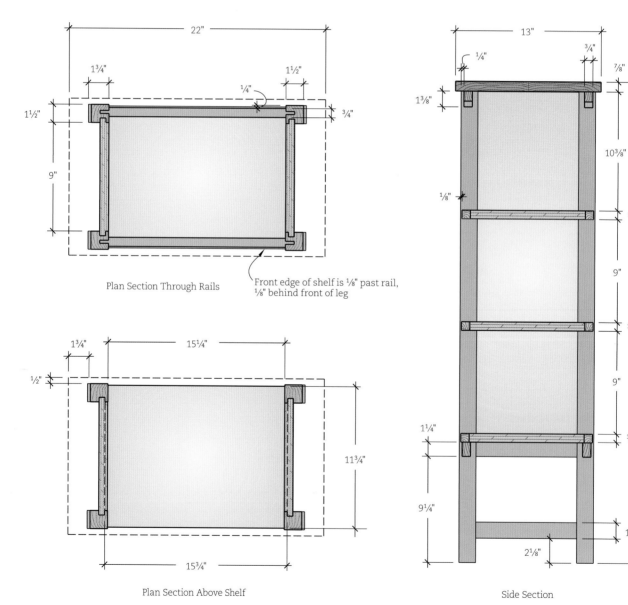

Plan Section Through Rails

Front edge of shelf is ⅛" past rail, ⅛" behind front of leg

Plan Section Above Shelf

Side Section

Illustrations by Robert W. Lang

Sure, you could set up your router table or table saw to cut the notches in the shelves. But a sharp backsaw works just as well.

The Shelves are Simple

Cut the shelves to finished size and mark out the notch that needs to be cut in the corner of each shelf. This notch allows the shelves to wrap around the legs. You can rig up some fancy setup with your router table to do this, but I prefer using a backsaw for such a simple task (see the photo above).

Now fit your shelves in the dados and make any adjustments necessary using a block plane or chisel. When everything is fitting nice and snug, it's time to cut the mortise-and-tenon joints that hold everything together.

I usually cut my tenons using a dado stack or a tenon saw. When it comes to mortises, I usually choose to drill them out on the drill press or fire up the hollow-chisel mortising machine.

Details Lighten the Load

With the tenons and mortises milled, it's time to make a few cuts that visually will slim this chunky box a bit.

The first order of business is cutting the curve on the top rails. Mark the curve using the diagrams and a flexible piece of scrap wood. Cut the curve using a coping saw and clean up the saw marks using a spokeshave or sandpaper.

Now cut the tapers on the legs using the diagrams as a guide. I cut the tapers using my band saw and cleaned up the cuts with a smoothing plane. Keep the offcuts because they are useful when gluing the case together at the end of the project.

Now sand or plane down all your parts and glue up the side assemblies. In order to attach the top, screw the cleats to the top edge of your side assemblies and bore a couple holes through the cleats. Break all the edges of your parts with #120-grit sandpaper.

Now comes an important decision. You can go ahead and assemble the case and then finish it. Or you can tape off the joints, finish the individual parts and then assemble the case. I took the latter course.

I kept the finish simple on this piece. I wiped on Minwax's "red mahogany 225" stain on all the parts. This stain is available at most home-center stores; 8 ounces will cost you less than $3. Allow the stain to dry overnight.

The next day, apply a few coats of your film finish of choice. I sprayed M.L. Campbell's Magnalac precatalyzed lacquer (satin sheen) using a HVLP spray system. Sand between the second and third coats with #320-grit stearated sandpaper. Remove the tape from the tenons and then glue up the individual parts of the cabinet. Use the falloff pieces from cutting the leg tapers to clamp the lower part of the case squarely.

If you haven't figured it out yet, magazine cabinets aren't much good for storing modern magazines (unless you stacked them flat). But they do make handy bookshelves — especially for antique volumes.

Once I set the cabinet in place next to my fireplace and loaded it up with books, I took a second look at the picture of the original in the 1910 Gustav Stickley catalog. Someone in his art department should have been fired for butchering that photo. This is a nice piece.

Now fit your parts together and tune up the notches in the shelves with a sharp chisel so you get a tight fit between the sides and the shelves.

A spokeshave cleans up your saw cuts on the top rails quickly. After working with the fancy Leigh jig, it's a relief to pick up a tool that's simpler than I am.

Most people don't notice the tapers on the legs. (My wife didn't, and she has a sharp enough eye to always find my car keys.) The tapers are critical, however. You definitely would notice their absence.

CHAPTER SEVEN

Stickley Bookcase

by Laurie McKichan

When I'm designing furniture, I often turn to the Arts and Crafts era for inspiration. I love this style. It's simple, but elegant. When a client commissioned me to build a small bookcase, I knew exactly what to start with: a photograph of a piece built by L. & J. G. Stickley around 1904.

This Stickley bookcase was perfect for my clients' modern condo. They wanted a bookcase with an open back, so it could be accessed from both sides and used as a room divider. I changed the Stickley piece's dimensions and design a bit, but kept the distinctive look of its side panels.

As it turned out, my clients moved just as I was completing their bookcase. They didn't need a divider in their new living room, but they did need a piece to fit behind their sofa. The bookcase was a natural. It's proven to be a very versatile design!

Materials and Tools

I built this bookcase from quartersawn white oak, the same kind of wood that was used to build most Arts and Crafts furniture. This wood's most prominent feature is its ray fleck, but some quartersawn boards have much

Begin by routing double mortises in the legs. I'm using a Leigh FMT Pro, a jig which has templates of various sizes to guide the router. Many types of shop-made jigs can make these joints, too.

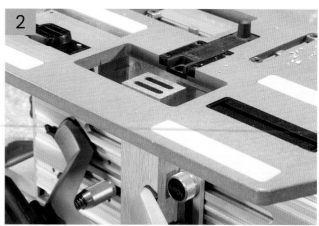

Rout similar mortises in the ends of the rails. This jig holds work both horizontally and vertically.

Mill some long, thin pieces to make loose tenons. Round the edges of these pieces to fit the mortises.

Cut the tenon stock into short pieces and glue them into the rails.

better-looking figure than others. Before I got started, I set aside the best boards for the side panels and the top.

The double tenons I used on this bookcase can be tricky to machine. I've found that the easiest method is to make them as loose pieces, like dowels or biscuits. This requires a lot of accurately machined mortises, made with a plunge router. You can make your own jigs to guide the router, but I used the Leigh FMT, which is designed for this kind of work (see Sources, page 54).

Make the Joints

Begin by making the legs (B). Cut them to final size and mark the best sides to face front and out. Rout all the mortises in the legs (Photo 1 and Fig. D).

Mill all the rails (C, D, E, F and K). Be sure to trim all of the side rails (E and F) and the anti-racking rails

(K) to the same length. Rout mortises in their ends, to match the mortises in the legs (Photo 2).

Make loose tenons (M, N, P and Q) to fit the mortises. They're all the same thickness, but have different widths. Make each batch of tenons from one piece that's at least 12" long (shorter pieces aren't safe to mill).

Note that the tenons for the front and back upper rails are ⅛" narrower than their corresponding mortises. This important detail requires a little explanation. These mortises are horizontal, rather than vertical. The tenons are narrower than the mortises so you can adjust the position of the rails side to side later on, to accommodate the length of the anti-racking rails (K). If the tenons were exactly the same width as the mortises, you'd have to mill the joints very precisely so that all the parts would fit together. While that's not out of the question, my approach – leaving some room for adjustment – is much easier.

Round the edges of the tenon stock on the router table (Photo 3). Cut the stock into short pieces and glue the tenons into the rails (Photo 4). On the front and back upper rails (the ones with the narrower tenons), glue the tenons in the middle of the mortises.

Build the Sides

Mill the side panels (G), but leave them 1" extra long. Assemble the sides, without glue, and measure the distance between the rails (Photo 5). Cut the panels to this exact length (it's best to take off a little at a time, until they fit perfectly). Disassemble the sides.

Cut three biscuit slots in the ends of the panels and in the upper and lower side rails (Photo 6 and Fig. A). Pre-finish the edges of the side rails that have the biscuit slots. The panels will contract when the weather is dry; pre-finishing prevents this shrinkage from revealing unfinished wood.

Glue the sides together, all in one shot. I use Titebond Extend for complicated assemblies like this. Its open time is longer than the open time of most yellow glues, so I don't have to rush as fast. Start by gluing the side panels to the rails – the joints that have three biscuits. Apply glue only to the center slots, and leave the outer ones dry. This will allow the panel to shrink and swell without being restrained by glue.

After the sides are glued, plane or sand the top rails and legs so they're even, if necessary. Cut a pair of biscuit slots on the inside edges of the top rails (Photo 7).

Assemble the Case

Drill holes and slots in the anti-racking rails for fastening the top (Fig. B). The ends of the rails have biscuit slots that are a bit unusual. These slots are more like grooves – they stop shy of one edge, and run all the way out of the other edge. This design will allow you to slide the piece over a biscuit, as you'll see later. The easiest way to make these long slots is to clamp the two anti-racking

Strong Joints Reduce Racking

Although this bookcase is relatively small, it's pretty heavy when it's loaded up. To handle that load, and to withstand being picked up and shoved around, it needs to be strong. Most bookcases have backs, which help stiffen what's essentially a box with an open front. My bookcase doesn't have a back, so I had to design joints that were very strong, without resorting to increasing the width of the rails. That would have spoiled the look of the bookcase.

Instead I made the rails quite thick (1¼"), and used mortise and tenon joints. Most of these joints have double tenons – two tenons side by side – rather than one large tenon. This strengthens the joints by doubling the area of their gluing surfaces. I made sure that the mortises in the legs didn't intersect each other, which could weaken the legs. Instead, the mortises are staggered.

I also added one unusual element to strengthen the case: a piece I call an "anti-racking" rail. There's one on each side of the bookcase just under the top. They reinforce the joint between the upper rails and the sides, to prevent the case from twisting, or racking.

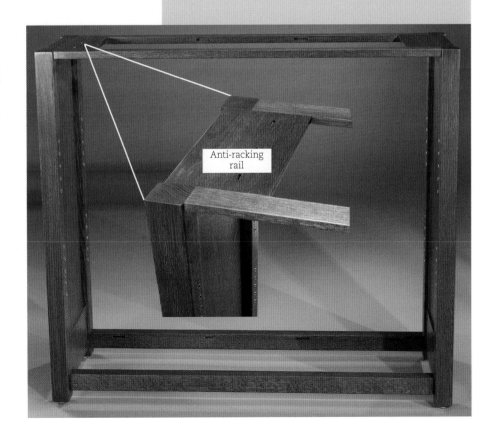

Anti-racking rail

Fig. A Exploded View

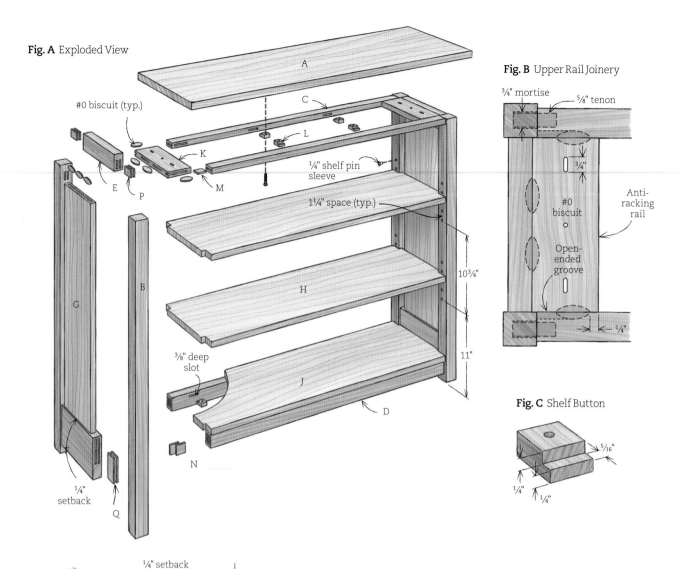

#0 biscuit (typ.)

A

C

L

K

E   P

M

1/4" shelf pin sleeve

1 1/4" space (typ.)

G

B

H

10 3/4"

11"

3/8" deep slot

J

D

1/4" setback

Q

N

Fig. B Upper Rail Joinery

3/4" mortise

5/8" tenon

3/4"

#0 biscuit

Anti-racking rail

Open-ended groove

1/4"

Fig. C Shelf Button

5/16"

1/4"

1/4"

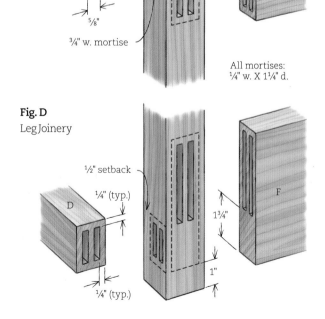

C

1/4"

1/4" setback

3/4"

E

5/8"

3/4" w. mortise

All mortises: 1/4" w. X 1 1/4" d.

Fig. D
Leg Joinery

1/2" setback

D

1/4" (typ.)

1 3/4"

1"

1/4" (typ.)

F

Cutting List Overall Dimensions: 36 5/8" H x 45 1/2" W x 13 1/4" D

PART	ITEM	DIMENSIONS (INCHES)			QTY.
		T	W	L	
A	Top	7/8"	13 1/4"	45 1/2"	1
B	Legs	1 3/4"	1 3/4"	35 3/4"	4
C	Upper rail, front/back	3/4"	1 1/2"	38"	2
D	Lower rail, front/back	1 1/4"	1 3/4"	38"	2
E	Upper rail, side	1 1/4"	2"	9"	2
F	Lower rail, side	1 1/4"	5"	9"	2
G	Side panel	3/4"	7 1/2"	27 3/4"	2
H	Shelf, middle/top	3/4"	12"	38 7/8"	2
J	Shelf, bottom	3/4"	12"	38 3/8"	1
K	Rail, anti-racking	5/8"	3 1/2"	9"	2
L	Button	1/2"	1"	1 5/16"	10
M	Tenons, upper rail	1/4"	5/8"	2 1/2" (a, b)	4
N	Tenons, lower rail	1/4"	1 1/4"	2 1/2" (c)	8
P	Tenons, upper rail, side	1/4"	1"	2 1/2" (c)	8
Q	Tenons, lower rail, side	1/4"	3"	2 1/2" (c)	8

Assemble the bookcase's side, without glue. Measure the distance between the rails. Cut the side panels to this length.

Cut biscuit slots in the ends of the side panels. Glue the sides together.

Plane the top of each side so the rails and legs are flush. Cut biscuit slots on the inside face of the top rails.

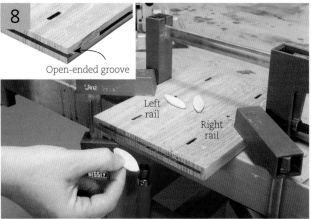

Open-ended groove

Left rail

Right rail

Make two "anti-racking" rails, and clamp them together. Cut a series of biscuit slots in their ends, to make one long groove. When you separate the pieces, the groove will run out the side of each piece (see inset).

rails together (Photo 8), and make a number of regular plunge cuts at each end.

Cut single biscuit slots in the upper front and back rails to receive the anti-racking rails. Glue biscuits in these slots, and carefully remove any glue squeeze-out.

One more thing before getting ready to glue: Rout slots on the inside faces of all four front and back rails to receive the wood buttons (L) that will fasten the top and lower shelf (Fig. A). Make the buttons from a long piece of stock (Fig. C).

You're ready for the big glue-up. First, place biscuits—without glue—into the ends of the anti-racking rails, and clamp these rails between the upper rails (Photo 9). Position the anti-racking rails so they project about ¼" beyond the ends of the upper rails. Use a framing square to align the ends of the upper rails.

Glue the case (Photo 10). Again, with so many pieces to handle, using glue with a longer open time will really

help. Before the glue dries, loosen the clamps that hold the anti-racking rails and slide these rails back an inch or so, to ensure that they aren't inadvertently glued in place. When the glue dries, remove the anti-racking rails. Spread glue on the ends and sides of these rails, slide them back in place (Photo 11), and clamp them to the sides.

Finishing Up

Glue up the shelves (H & J) and top (A), and cut them to final size. Notch the shelves so there's a ¹/₁₆" gap between the shelves and the end panels (so you can drop the shelves in place), and a similar gap between the shelves and the legs (so the shelves have room to expand in width). Make a plywood template for spacing the shelf pins and drill their holes. I use brass sleeves (see Sources) to line the shelf pin holes; the sleeves add a nice decorative touch to the bookcase. Install the sleeves after the piece is finished.

9

Anti-racking
rail

Open-ended
groove

Cut biscuit slots in the upper rails to receive the anti-racking rails. Clamp the parts together using biscuits, but no glue. Align the ends of the upper rails with each other.

10

Glue the case together. Slide out the anti-racking rails before the glue dries.

11

Spread glue on the ends and inner edge of the anti-racking rails, and slide them back in place. Clamp the rails to the sides.

I use a three-step finish on white oak. First, I apply a yellow dye (see Sources). Next, I wipe on one or two coats of Bartley's Jet Mahogany gel stain, followed by three applications of Bartley's gel varnish.

After the finish is dry, fasten the lower shelf and the top to the case (Photo 12). Center the top on the case. Using a spacer, leave a ⅛" gap between the button and the rails, to allow the shelf and top to expand when the humidity is high. In addition to the buttons, secure the top with screws that go through the anti-racking rails.

Sources

Leigh Industries, www.leighjigs.com, (800) 663-8932, FMT Pro, $1,189; Super FMT, $599.

Widget Mfg. Co., WidgetCo.com, (800) 877-9270, ¼" Antique Brass Shelf Pins, #1-250-ATQ-S, $0.16 each; ¼" Antique Brass Shelf Pin Sleeves, #1-250-ATQ-G, $0.16 each.

Homestead Finishing Products, www.homesteadfinishingproducts.com, TransFast Lemon Yellow powdered dye stain, water soluble, #3287, $35.70/ 4 oz.

Woodworker's Supply, www.woodworker.com, (800) 645-9292, Bartley's Jet Mahogany Gel Stain, $24.99/ qt; Gel Varnish, $24.99/qt.

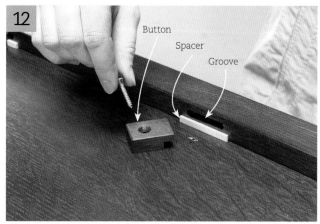

12

Button

Spacer

Groove

Fasten the lower shelf and top. I like using shop-made wooden buttons, which fit into grooves in the rails. Buttons add a classy look–although you have to get on your hands and knees to see them!

CHAPTER EIGHT

Bow-front Bookcase

by Randy Johnson

This bookcase combines straightforward joinery and materials in a design that won't overwhelm your budget or your room. Yet its deep shelves provide plenty of room for oversize books or a place to display your collectibles. The thick, solid look of the center and end panels is achieved with a laminated plywood approach we call "sandwich" construction. This bookcase is fun to build, so let's get started.

Tools and Materials

You'll need a planer, jointer, table saw, band saw, belt sander, biscuit joiner, jigsaw, drill and finish sander, plus various hand tools, to complete this project.

We used uniform light birch plywood and select white birch lumber for the main parts of the bookcase. These materials have an overall white/light color. For the top we used flame white birch that has a wonderful figure and grain pattern.

It takes about 2¾ sheets of plywood and 30 board feet of lumber to build this bookcase. The wood costs about $350. If you use natural birch instead, it will cost about half as much to build. Natural birch contains darker heartwood and is what you find on the racks at most home centers.

Start with the Legs

Joint, plane and cut the legs (A) to final size. Then band saw and finish-sand the tapered feet (Photo 1). Note that the center legs and the end legs have different sides tapered (Fig. A, Detail 1, page 57). The legs are done first because the center sandwiched panel will be made to match the thickness of the legs (Photo 3).

Build the Sandwiched Panels

Saw the plywood parts for the center partition and the end panels (parts B, C and D, and Photo 2). See the Cutting List, page 65, for dimensions and the Plywood

Sandwich Construction

Sandwich construction uses readily available thicknesses of plywood to create thicker panels. It also lets you produce a panel that has two very good-looking sides because the best side of each piece of plywood faces outward.

There are two basic ways to create a sandwich panel. The first is to simply glue two pieces of plywood back to back. This is the approach we used for the end panels in this bookcase (see photo, below left). This approach works well for cabinet parts that will be fastened to other cabinet parts, such as the ends of this bookcase, which are biscuited and glued to the subtop and the bottom shelf. The reason for fastening these end panels is because the plywood parts that make up the panels are different thicknesses (¼" and ¾"), so

there is a risk of warping. However, if the sandwiched plywood parts are the same thickness, the chance of warping is greatly reduced. Such panels can even be used where they won't be fastened down, as for cabinet doors or adjustable shelves.

The second way to create a sandwiched panel is to use a center core with a layer of plywood glued to each side (see photo, below right). The center core can be either a lumber frame or another piece of plywood. The lumber-frame approach has the advantage of letting you produce a panel of precise thickness that weighs less than one made with a plywood core. Either core will make a sandwich that is resistant to warping.

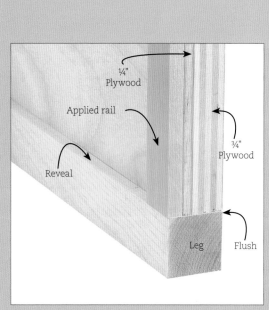

Gluing together a ¾" and a ¼" piece of plywood creates the end panels for this bookcase. This sandwiched panel is then trimmed to final size, and the legs and applied rails are added. The final result is an end panel that is flush on the inside with a frame-and-panel look on the outside.

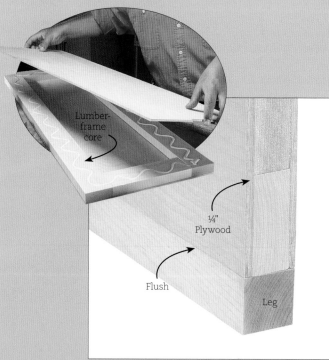

Gluing two pieces of ¼" plywood over a lumber-frame core creates the center panel for this bookcase. This creates an extra-thick but lightweight panel that is exactly the same thickness as the legs. With a lumber frame on the inside, you can custom-make panels any thickness you want.

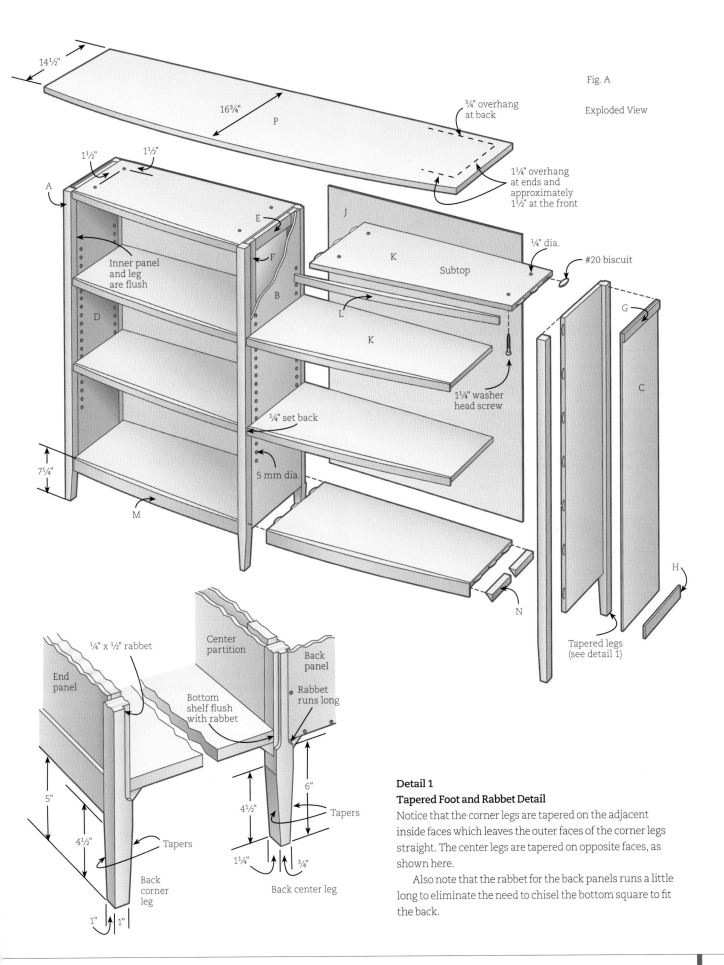

14½"

16¾"

P

¾" overhang
at back

Fig. A

Exploded View

1¼" overhang
at ends and
approximately
1½" at the front

1½"   1½"

A

Inner panel
and leg
are flush

D

E

F

B

J

K

Subtop

¼" dia.

#20 biscuit

L

K

1¼" washer
head screw

G

C

¼" set back

5 mm dia.

7¼"

M

N

H

Tapered legs
(see detail 1)

End
panel

¼" x ½" rabbet

Center
partition

Back
panel

Bottom
shelf flush
with rabbet

Rabbet
runs long

5"

4½"

Tapers

Back
corner
leg

6"

4½"

Tapers

1¼"   ¾"

Back center leg

1"   1"

Detail 1
Tapered Foot and Rabbet Detail
Notice that the corner legs are tapered on the adjacent
inside faces which leaves the outer faces of the corner legs
straight. The center legs are tapered on opposite faces, as
shown here.

Also note that the rabbet for the back panels runs a little
long to eliminate the need to chisel the bottom square to fit
the back.

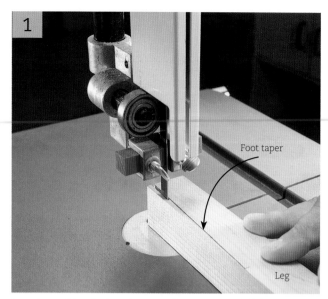

Start by making the legs, because the center sandwiched panel will be made to match them in thickness. After band-sawing the tapered foot at the bottom of the legs, sand the taper smooth.

Saw the plywood parts for the sandwiched end and center panels. These parts should be cut oversize at this point. They will be trimmed to final size after they are sandwiched together.

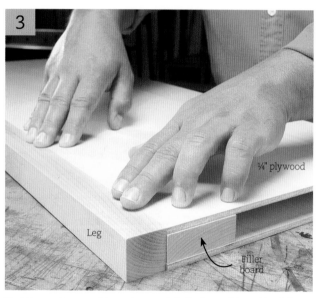

Test the center panel to make sure it is flush on either side of the leg. Adjust the thickness of the filler boards as needed.

Glue and clamp together the sandwiched panels. The center panel (shown here) uses filler boards. The end panels are just two pieces of plywood sandwiched together.

Layout (Fig. F) for a recommended cutting plan. Pay attention to which side of the plywood looks best. You want to pick the best side to face out on the glued-up sandwiched panels.

Next make the fillers (E and F) for the center partition and check that they're the correct thickness (Photo 3). It's tempting to use ¾" plywood for these fillers because ¾ plus ¼ plus ¼ equals 1¼, right?

Not when it comes to plywood. Plywood is often ¹⁄₃₂" or more thinner than its specified thickness. This can have a noticeable effect on the final thickness of a sandwiched panel.

Proceed with gluing together the plywood parts that form the sandwiched center and end panels (Photo 4). When the glue is dry, trim the sandwiched panels to final size (Photos 5 and 6).

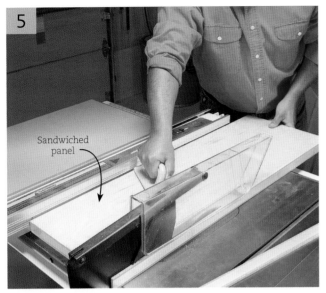

Trim the glued-up sandwiched panels to final width. Cut a little off each edge so both edges are straight and parallel to each other.

Saw the sandwiched panels to final length. This is easy to accomplish with the help of a tablesaw sled. Cut a little off both ends so they are parallel to each other and square to the edges of the panels.

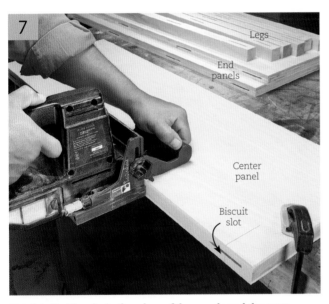

Cut slots for biscuits in the edges of the panels and the corresponding sides of the legs. The biscuits help keep the legs and panels aligned when they are glued together.

Glue and clamp the legs to the panels. The center panel is flush on both sides of the legs but the end panels are flush only to the inside of the legs. It's not necessary to put glue on the biscuits since they are mainly for alignment.

Add the Legs

Use biscuits and glue to attach the legs to the sandwiched panels (Fig. A, Photos 7 and 8). Pay close attention to the orientation of the tapered foot on the legs when you are cutting the biscuit slots (Fig. A, Detail 1). It's easy to make a mistake here and cut slots in the wrong face of the legs. Also note that the legs are flush with both sides of the center panel but are flush only with the inside of the end panels.

After the legs are attached to the end panels, add the applied top and bottom rails (parts G and H, Fig. A). Complete the three panels by routing the rabbets in the back legs (Photo 9 and Detail 1). The ¼" plywood backs (J) will fit into these rabbets once the case is assembled.

Make the Curved Shelves

The curved front shelves and subtops start out as rectangular plywood parts (K) and are tapered on the front edge using a tapering sled (Fig. B) on your table saw (Photo 10). To make left and right tapers on the same sled, cut four of these parts best-side up and four best-side down. This gives you three left shelves and three right shelves, all with their best side up, plus a left and right subtop.

Next, glue the solid-wood edging (L and M) to the tapered edge of the shelves and subtops (Photo 11 and Fig. C). Pay attention that the edging is flush with the good (top) side of the shelves. It doesn't matter which face the edging overhangs on the subtops, just be sure

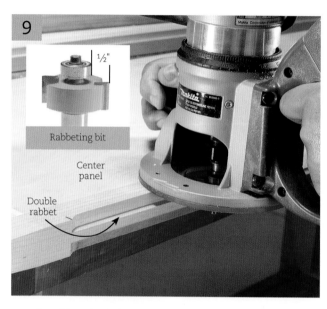

Rout the rabbets in the back of the rear legs. The plywood back fits into this rabbet once the case is assembled. The center leg gets two rabbets and the side legs get only one rabbet.

Taper the front edge on the shelves using a table saw tapering sled. This is necessary because the bowed front of the bookcase makes the shelves wider at one end than the other.

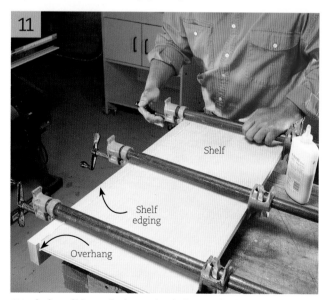

Attach the solid-wood edge to the shelves and subtops. Let the ends of the wood edging run a little long. After the glue is dry, use a handsaw to trim the overhanging ends flush with the ends of the shelves.

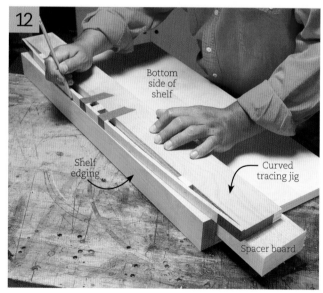

Use a tracing jig to draw a curved line on the bottom side of the shelf edging. Drawing it on the bottom side makes band sawing easier (Photo 13). Use a spacer board to support the tracing jig while drawing.

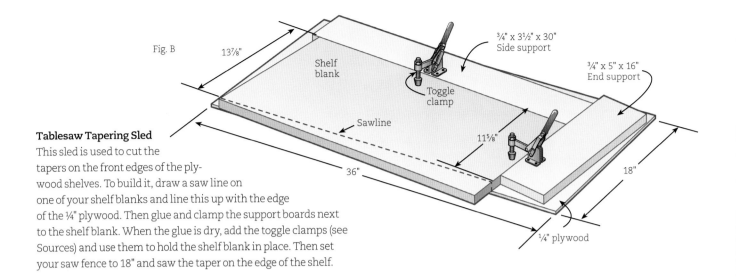

Tablesaw Tapering Sled

This sled is used to cut the tapers on the front edges of the plywood shelves. To build it, draw a saw line on one of your shelf blanks and line this up with the edge of the ¼" plywood. Then glue and clamp the support boards next to the shelf blank. When the glue is dry, add the toggle clamps (see Sources) and use them to hold the shelf blank in place. Then set your saw fence to 18" and saw the taper on the edge of the shelf.

Fig. B

13⅞"

Shelf blank

¾" x 3½" x 30" Side support

Toggle clamp

¾" x 5" x 16" End support

Sawline

11⅝"

36"

18"

¼" plywood

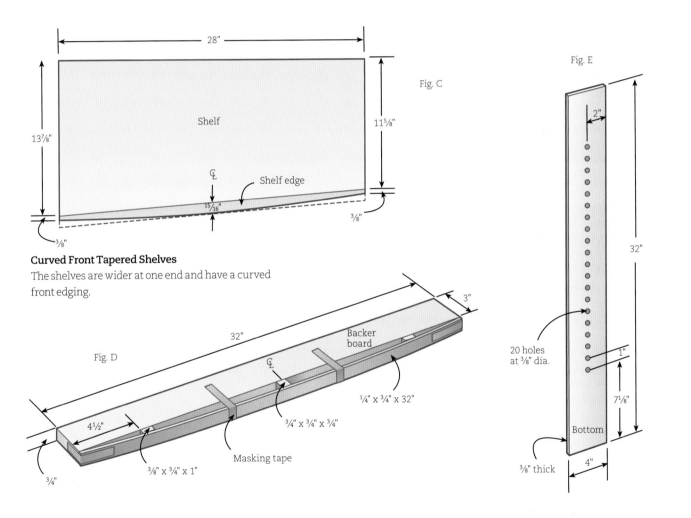

Fig. C

28"

Shelf

13⅞"

11⅝"

C̶L̶

Shelf edge

15⁄16"

⅜"

⅜"

Curved Front Tapered Shelves

The shelves are wider at one end and have a curved front edging.

Fig. D

32"

Backer board

3"

C̶L̶

¼" x ¾" x 32"

¾" x ¾" x ¾"

Masking tape

4½"

⅜" x ¾" x 1"

¾"

Curved Tracing Jig

This jig is used to draw the curves on both the shelves and the bookcase top. The small spacer blocks can be glued to the backer board and then the thin wood strip can be held in place with masking tape.

Fig. E

2"

32"

20 holes at ⅜" dia.

1"

7⅛"

Bottom

⅜" thick

4"

Shelf Pin Drilling Guide

Mark the bottom of the guide so you don't accidentally flip it over and end up with holes that don't line up.

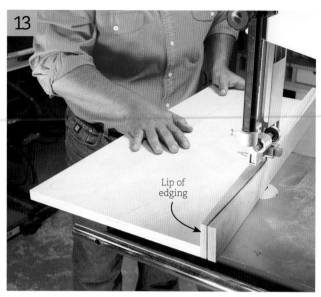

Use a bandsaw to cut the curve into the shelf edging with the lip of the edging pointing up.

Sand the curved edging smooth. Start with a belt sander and finish up with an orbital sander or by hand.

you make one left and one right. Use the curved tracing jig (Fig. D) as a guide to draw the curves on the bottom of the edging of the shelves and subtop (Photo 12). Then band saw and sand the edging to final shape (Photos 13 and 14).

Assemble the Bookcase in Stages

Start by cutting biscuit slots in the ends of the bottom shelves and subtops, and the joining surfaces of the center and end panels (Fig. A). Remember that the shelves are flush with the rabbet at the back of the legs (Detail 1) and set back ¼" from the front of the legs (Fig. A).

Gluing and clamping these parts together is a two-stage process (Photos 15 and 16). Practice each stage without glue to make sure the parts line up correctly and to get a feel for how they go together. Get a helper to assist with holding the parts. Make sure the case is square before leaving it to dry.

After the case is glued up and dry, flip it over on its top and add glue blocks (N) to the under side (Photo 17). Glue blocks are an easy way to add strength to the case. After the glue is dry, turn the cabinet right-side up and drill the shelf-pin holes using a self-centering bit (see Sources, page 66) and a shop-made drilling guide (Photo 18 and Fig. E).

Now is a good time to take the four remaining shelves back to the table saw and cut ¹/₁₆" off one end of each shelf. It doesn't matter which end, because you're just trying to provide some clearance so they're easy to install and remove from the cabinet. A regular table saw sled makes this step easy and safe. Add a ¼" plywood spacer under the bottom of the shelf to accommodate

the overhang of the edging and cut the shelves good-side up. This way, if any chipping occurs, it will be on the under side of the shelf.

Complete this phase of assembly by attaching the plywood back panels (J) (Photo 19).

Make the Solid-Wood Top

After selecting the boards for the curved top (P), plane them to thickness and joint the edges square. Use boards long and wide enough to produce a glued-up top that is about 1" oversize in length and width. You will cut the top to final size after these boards are glued together.

Cut biscuit slots about every 6" along the joining edges. Keep the slots in a couple of inches from the ends so you don't expose them when trimming the top to final length. Biscuits help keep the boards aligned during clamping, but don't expect to have perfectly flush joints everywhere. You will most likely have a few ridges that will need to be scraped or sanded. Also, don't worry if the top develops a little twist after it's glued up. Our top ended up about ½" high at one corner but easily pulled flat when we screwed it onto the bookcase.

After you have the boards for the top glued up, cut it to final length. Next, mark the final width at the middle and the ends and use the tracing jig to draw the curve (Photo 20). Cut the curve with a jigsaw and sand it smooth. Attach the top to the subtop with washer head screws (Photo 21).

Finishing

Now that you have the bookcase all together you get to take it apart for finishing (Photo 22). Remove the top,

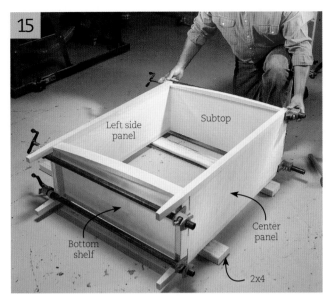

15

Left side panel

Subtop

Bottom shelf

Center panel

2x4

Glue and clamp together one half of the bookcase first. It's a good idea to test-assemble these parts before you use glue. Propping up the cabinet on a couple of 2x4s makes it easy to check that the parts are correctly aligned on the back edges.

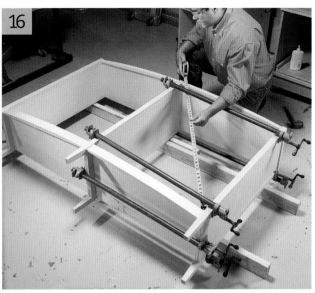

16

Add the second section of the bookcase once the glue in the first section is completely dry. Again, check that everything is square before leaving it to dry.

17

Glue block

Flip over the bookcase and add glue blocks to the bottom. They add an extra measure of rigidity and strength to the legs and case.

18

Self-centering bit

Drilling template

Flush with leg

Bottom

Drill 5mm holes for the shelf pins using a self-centering bit and a drilling template. Align the template flush with the front legs and the rabbets at the rear.

the adjustable shelves and the backs. This makes finishing the parts easier and putting it back together simple, since you know all the parts fit correctly. We used a clear satin varnish on our bookcase. It brought out the grain and gave it a warm natural look.

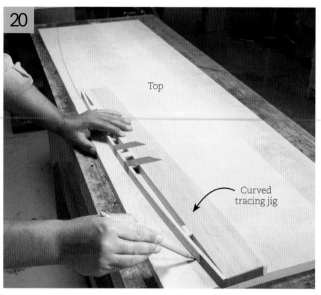

Attach the back with pan head screws. Drilling pilot holes first makes driving the screws a lot easier. The back is now removable, which makes finishing easier later on.

Draw the curve on the top of the bookcase using the same tracing jig you used for the shelves. Draw one side of the curve first and then the other.

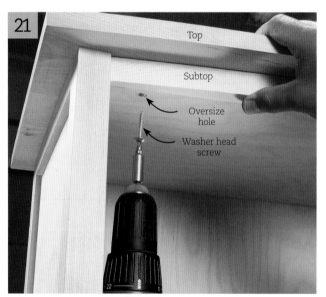

Attach the top using washer head screws. The holes in the subtop are oversize to allow for seasonal movement of the solid-wood top.

Disassemble the bookcase and finish it with your favorite finish. A clear satin vanish looks great on white birch.

Washer head screws are commonly used to attach drawer fronts to drawer boxes, but they also work great for attaching tops to cabinets. The large washer head holds tight without digging into the plywood. Once you've tried them you'll find many uses for them. They're available in 1¼", 1½" and 1¾" lengths (see Sources).

Fig. F

Plywood Layout

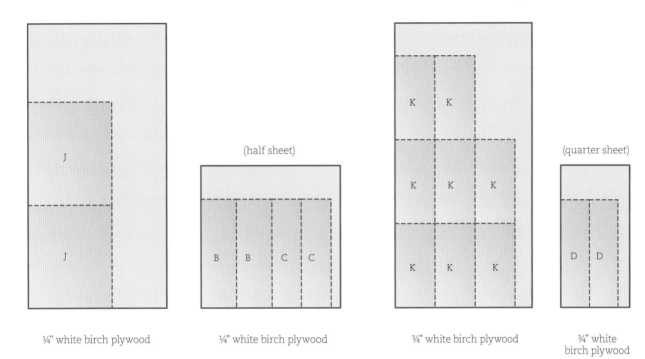

¼" white birch plywood   ¼" white birch plywood   ¾" white birch plywood   ¾" white birch plywood

Cutting List   **Overall Dimensions 62¼" W x 42" H x 16¾" D**

PART	ITEM	QTY.	DIMENSIONS (INCHES)			MATERIAL	COMMENTS
			T	**W**	**L**		
A	Legs	6	1¼"	1¼"	41¼"	6/4 birch	
B	Center partition panels	2	¼"	12¼"	36¼"	birch plywood	Add ½" to width and length for rough sawing
C	Outer end panels	2	¼"	10"	36¼"	birch plywood	Add ½" to width and length for rough sawing
D	Inner end panels	2	¾"	10"	36¼"	birch plywood	Add ½" to width and length for rough sawing
E	Short filler boards	2	⅞"	2½"	7¼"	birch	Plane thickness to fit (see Photo 3)
F	Long filler boards	2	⅞"	2½"	36¼"	birch	Plane thickness to fit (see Photo 3)
G	Applied top rails	2	5⁄16"	1"	10"	birch	Plane thickness to be flush with side of legs
H	Applied bottom rails	2	5⁄16"	2¼"	10"	birch	Plane thickness to be flush with side of legs
J	Back panels	2	¼"	29"	34¾"	birch plywood	
K	Tapered shelves and subtops	8	¾"	14"	28"	birch plywood	Rough width, finished width is 13⅞" at wide end and 11⅝" at narrow end
L	Edging for shelves and subtop	6	1"	1"	29"	5/4 birch	Rough length, trim to final length after
M	Edging for bottom shelves	2	1"	2¼"	29"	5/4 birch	gluing to shelves and subtops
N	Glue blocks	8	1"	1"	3½"	5/4 birch	
P	Curved top	1	¾"	16¾"	62¼"	4/4 flame birch	Glue up from narrower boards

Sources

Woodworkers Hardware, (800) 383-0130
www.wwhardware.com
1" washer head screws, #SCLP8X1; $4 per 100
1¼" washer head screws, #SCLP8X114; $5 per 100
1½" washer head screws, #SCLP8X112; $4 per 100
5mm steel shelf pins, #G402BN; $3 per 20

Woodworkers Supply, (800) 645-9292
www.woodworker.com
Rabbeting router bit, #819-647; $25.99 ea.
Toggle clamp, #173-001; $11.59 ea.

Lee Valley, (800) 871-8158
www.leevalley.com
5mm self-centering drill bit, #04J05.05; $8.50 ea.

CHAPTER NINE

Knockdown Bookcase

by David Thiel

The Arts & Crafts movement was part of an interesting social change in America – the advent of mail-order purchases. Catalogs from Sears, Roebuck and Co. and Montgomery Ward were all the rage, and many companies took their cue and offered their wares for sale through catalogs rather than set up expensive retail establishments throughout the country. While it was a great idea, it raised a difficult problem with furniture. The majority of space in any piece of furniture is air. While air is very light, it's also bulky and expensive to ship. So furniture makers perfected a style of furniture that continues today – knockdown furniture. Finished disassembled, the furniture could be shipped flat, then assembled by the owner. Through-tenons with tusks were the turn-of-the-20th-century answer, while hidden cam-locking hardware is the answer today.

Slanted Construction

This project is actually a very simple bookcase made challenging by slanting the sides. Many of the knockdown bookcases had straight sides, but why do things the easy way?

Start construction by preparing the panels for the sides and four shelves. If you aren't fortunate enough to have oak that's wide enough to make your sides using a single board, glue up the shelves or sides using two boards, but make sure the joint falls in the center of the finished panel. This is less important on the shelves; but since the sides come to a peak at the center, the joint becomes obvious if you're off the mark. Also, you can cut the top and bottom shelves to length, but leave the two center shelves long at this time. When the through-tenons are cut and fit, you can measure for the exact length of the center shelves.

Critical Pencil Lines

With the sides prepared, lay out the shelf locations, mortise locations and the overall shape in pencil on one

of them. To allow you to do a minimum of angled or beveled cutting on the pieces, the shelves all fit into ¾"-wide by ⅜"-deep dados cut at a 5° angle in the sides using the table saw. Because of this, the location of the shelves actually falls at an angle on the sides. A ¹⁄₁₆" difference in shelf height one way or the other won't dramatically

After carefully laying out the shelf locations, use a dado stack (set at a 5° angle) and the saw's miter gauge to cut the angled dados.

This simple scrap-wood jig made angled mortises a fairly simple task.

affect the use of the bookcase, but you must make sure that the dados are cut at the same locations on each side.

If you happen to have a sliding table on your table saw, you're in great shape. Most people don't, so the next best option to cut the angled dados is to use your miter gauge. If you don't have a substantial wooden fence attached to your gauge, now is a good time. A fence that is 18" to 24" long and about 3" high will work fine. You'll need to determine which way to orient the sides on your saw depending on the way the arbor of your saw tilts. With some of the cuts, the majority of the side will be supported by the miter gauge, and you can use your rip fence to guide your cut. When the larger section of the side will be between the blade and rip fence, this is an unsafe cut. The board can twist and bind against the blade and cause a kickback. Move the rip fence out of the way, mark the sides and make the next cuts with only the miter gauge fence. With the dados complete, swap the dado with a crosscut blade, and bevel the bottom edge of each side at that angle.

Angled Mortising

The next step is the through-mortises. For these to work correctly, they also need to be cut at a 5° angle, and they must fall directly in the dados you just cut on the saw. You could cut them by hand, but the 5° angle is tricky to maintain. You could also set up a mortiser to do the job, but I got a little smarter and came up with a router template.

By using a piece of ½" Baltic birch with a strip added beneath one end, I made a router template that would make cuts at a 5° angle. It takes some rearranging of the guide for the different cuts, but the results work rather well.

Careful layout lines are critical here. To make the 5° ramp, I used a scrap piece of ½" material for the back strip, nailed to the template 14" from the end. Check this dimension carefully on your materials to get as close to 5° as possible.

The rest is fairly simple. Check the offset on your router template guide from the bit, and add this to the ¾" x 2" dimension for the mortise. Mark that size on the template and use a drill and jigsaw to make a square hole.

Clamp the template in place over the mortise locations and cut your through-mortises using two or three depth settings. Depending on the router bit you're using, you may want to use a backing board behind the side to reduce tear-out. I used a jigsaw and chisel to square up the corners.

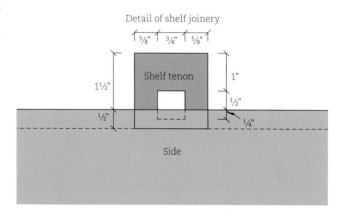

Detail of shelf joinery

With the sides clamped together and mounted in my vise, shaping the sides simply took some sanding and planing.

A close look at the wedged through-tenons shows the recess behind the side that allows the wedge to pull the sides tight.

Shaping up the Sides

The next step is to cut the sides to their "spade" shape. I used my band saw for most of this work, but used a jigsaw to cut the radii under the top shelf and the arch at the bottom. Cut a little wide of your layout lines, then clamp the sides together, aligning the sides by the shelf grooves on the inside surface. Plane and sand the sides to matching shapes.

Fitting the Through-Tenons

Now it's time to fit things together. Start by checking the fit of your shelves in the dados in the sides. Mine were a hair thick, so I was able to run them down on the planer to make an almost-perfect fit. Check the width of the bottom shelf against the width of the sides at the shelf location, now that the sides are shaped. Rip the shelf to size. Next, fit the shelf into the dado and, from the outside, mark the tenon location through the mortise on the end of the shelf. Remove the shelf and mark off the 2" length of each mortise, then head for the band saw again. The width of the tenons is the critical cut. The shoulder of the tenons should be neat, but that edge is buried in the side's dados, so it doesn't have to be perfect.

With the tenons cut for the bottom shelf, fit the shelf and sides together. You want a snug fit, but not too loose and not too tight. A chisel, file or rasp and some sanding should do the job. Take your time and get it right.

With the bottom shelf fit, check the dimensions on the top shelf, mark the tenons and repeat the fitting process. When that task is complete, fit the two center shelves and slide them into position. These shelves are designed to be left loose, but if they slide a little more than you like, a nail through the side into the center of the shelf will make a permanent solution, or you can drive a short wedge into the joint under the shelf for a temporary fix.

Tusks and the Home Stretch

To hold the top and bottom shelves in place – and the whole case together – disassemble the case and mark the ¾" x ¾" through-mortises on the shelf tenons as shown in the diagrams. I used my mortising machine to cut these holes. Another option is to use a drill press to cut the mortises and then square up the corners using a chisel.

Reassemble the case, then cut the eight tusks. Appropriately, the tusks should seat with their center at the shelf tenon. Fit the tusks as necessary, and tap them into place to make the whole case rigid. Now take it all apart one last time and sand everything to #150-grit.

For a finish, I used a simple dark-colored gel stain, wiping off the excess until I was happy with the depth of the color. I then top-coated the case with a couple of coats of lacquer.

The nicest thing about moving this bookcase is that after you knock out the eight tusks, everything fits in the trunk of a compact car.

Cutting List

NO.	ITEM	DIMENSIONS (INCHES)			NOTES
		T	W	L	
2	Sides	¾"	12"	48"*	
1	Bottom shelf	¾"	11⅛"	24½"	2" TBE
1	Top shelf	¾"	10"	19⅜"*	2" TBE
1	Third shelf	¾"	9⅞"	19"*	
1	Second shelf	¾"	8¹¹⁄₁₆"	17"*	
8	Tusks	¾"	¾"	3½"	

* Oversized for fitting; TBE = tenon, both ends

KNOCKDOWN BOOKCASE

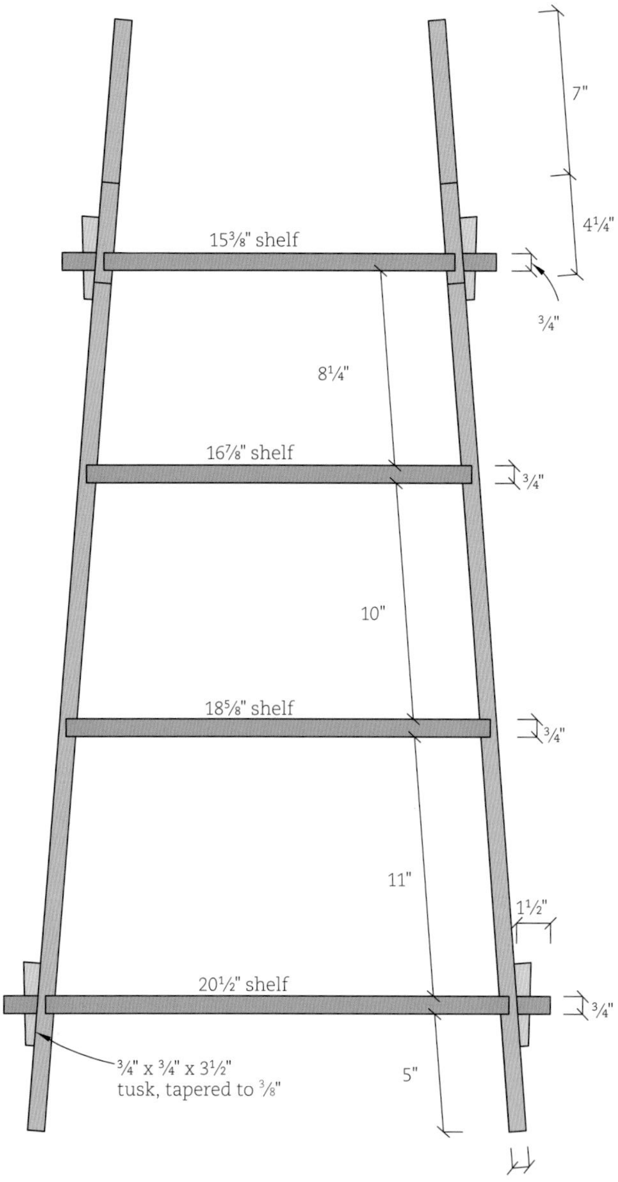
7"
4¼"
15⅜" shelf
¾"
8¼"
16⅞" shelf
¾"
10"
18⅝" shelf
¾"
11"
1½"
20½" shelf
¾"
¾" x ¾" x 3½"
tusk, tapered to ⅜"
5"
¾"

Elevation

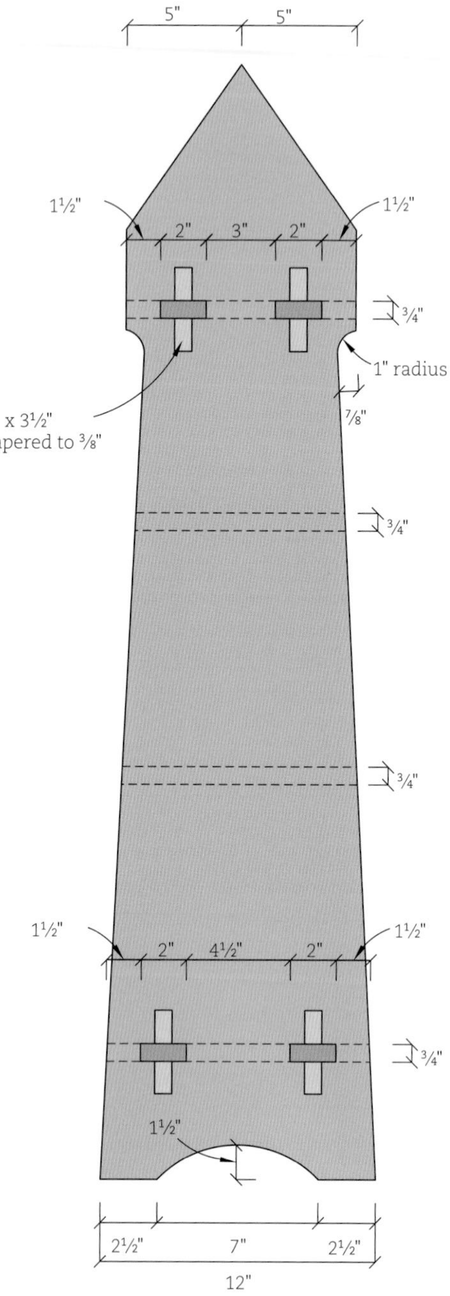
5"
5"
1½"
1½"
2"
3"
2"
¾"
1" radius
¾" x ¾" x 3½"
tusk, tapered to ⅜"
⅞"
¾"
¾"
1½"
1½"
2"
4½"
2"
¾"
1½"
2½"
7"
2½"
12"

Profile

CHAPTER TEN

Mid-Century Modern Bookcase

by Michael Crow

Mid-century modern design is enjoying a surge in popularity, and rightly so: Its clean lines and functional design make it practical and attractive, two traits evident in this bookcase by an unknown designer.

Its stark, geometric design shows modern roots while giving it a strong graphic presence. And because it looks good from both the front and back, it's perfect for dividing a space without completely partitioning it, making it a good match for the open-plan homes of the period, and of today.

Simple construction techniques underlie the sophisticated design: Rabbets in the leg assemblies capture the case, with its interior dividers and shelves joined by dados. The asymmetrical dividers are made from ½"-thick stock while the outer case is made from ¾"-thick material. The legs and rails are 1" thick. The varying thicknesses, and a ½" reveal of the case in the legs, add another subtle detail to the design.

The original case was executed in rosewood, but I opted for cherry finished with oil and shellac. It provides a warmth similar to rosewood without the expense. Too, the design lends itself to a variety of materials, so pick your materials to suit your décor.

Following the original, I built the case from sheet goods (the legs and rails are solid cherry), but there's no reason to choose sheet goods over solid wood. While plywood does require edge-banding, you'll likely spend the same amount of time gluing up narrower solid stock to produce the wide boards required for the project, so let your preference and working style guide your choice of material.

Edge-banding Two Ways

Because it simplifies cleaning glue squeeze-out, I prefer to pre-finish my parts when a design allows it. That's the approach I took here for the case interior, wiping

on a coat of boiled linseed oil, followed by padding on a couple of coats of blonde shellac.

Rip the ¾" and ½" plywood to 10¼" (which allows for ⅛"-thick edge-banding on both sides to produce 10½"-wide panels). Then apply the boiled linseed oil and

Edge banding two ways: clamp and caul, or use masking tape. For either approach, make sure your banding is wide enough to stand slightly proud of both faces of the board.

A trim router equipped with a flush-cutting bit makes quick work of trimming the edge-banding – but so can a block plane or smoothing plane (though you need to take care to avoid gouging the thin veneer face).

first coat of shellac. With the panels ripped and pre-finished, you're ready for edge-banding.

You can use commercial veneer tape and iron it to the edges of your plywood, but ripping your own banding gives you enough thickness to round or chamfer your finished edges. That looks nicer, and it makes the banding blend better with the sheet stock.

While it's tempting to set the fence for a narrow cut for ripping, you'll avoid the risk of the narrow stock jamming in the throat plate if you position the fence to produce a strong $\frac{1}{8}$" offcut, and reset the fence after every pass.

After ripping my banding, I planed one face smooth for gluing, then applied it to my plywood. I sized the edge of the plywood by brushing on a thin layer of glue, letting it sit for a minute for the long-grain plies to absorb glue, then applying another thin coat before aligning the banding to the sheet-good edges.

You can use a clamp and cauls to secure the banding while the glue dries, or you can use masking tape, scraping away any glue squeeze-out after it gels.

Once the glue is dry, cut the banding flush with the plywood. A trim router equipped with a flush-cutting bit

is designed for this work. The hand-tool alternative is a sharp plane set for a shallow cut.

Dados Join the Interior

The case interior is joined with $\frac{1}{4}$" x $\frac{1}{4}$" dados, stopped about $\frac{1}{2}$" from the edges of the boards. A simple plywood jig (shown below, left) guides the router for making these cuts.

Mark the location of the dados, align the cut in the fence with your marks, position the router, plunge and plow. Note that where two shelves line up on either side of a divider, the dados will cut all the way through the plywood, leaving solid stock only at either end of the cut.

Take care when handling the unassembled $\frac{1}{2}$"-thick dividers to avoid breaking the workpiece – or set your router a little shallow for these cuts, then trim the corresponding tenons to fit.

This simple jig holds the router base in position and guides it while cutting stopped dados. Align the bit at the start of the cut ($\frac{1}{2}$" in from the edge), plunge, then plow.

I used a router with a rabbeting bit to cut $\frac{1}{4}$"-thick tenons on the divider and shelf ends.

A simple plywood fence clamped flush with the end of the board guides the 45° chamfer bit (take multiple passes) for clean miters. The fence should extend past the edges of the board, and the inside edge of the board should face up.

Cutting List

NO.	ITEM	DIMENSIONS (INCHES)			MATERIAL
		T	W	L	
2	Case bottom/top	¾"	10½"*	35¾"	Plywood
2	Case side panels	¾"	10½"	38¾"	Plywood
1	Long shelf	½"	10½"*	17⅜"	Plywood
1	Medium-long shelf	½"	10½"*	10½"	Plywood
5	Medium shelves	½"	10½"*	8¹¹⁄₁₆"	Plywood
1	Short shelf	½"	10½"*	7⅜"	Plywood
2	Tall vertical dividers	½"	10½"*	37¾"	Plywood
1	Short vertical divider	½"	10½"*	28⁵⁄₁₆"	Plywood
2	Side frame rails	1"	1½"	12"	Cherry
4	Legs	1"	1½"	48½"	Cherry
DRAWER					
1	bottom	¼"	6⅜"	9½"	Plywood
2	Front/back	¾"	6⅞"	6¹⁵⁄₁₆"	Maple
2	Sides	½"	6¹⁵⁄₁₆"	10"	Poplar

*Includes ⅛"-thick solid edge-banding on both edges

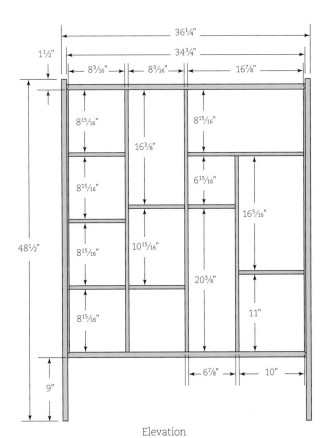

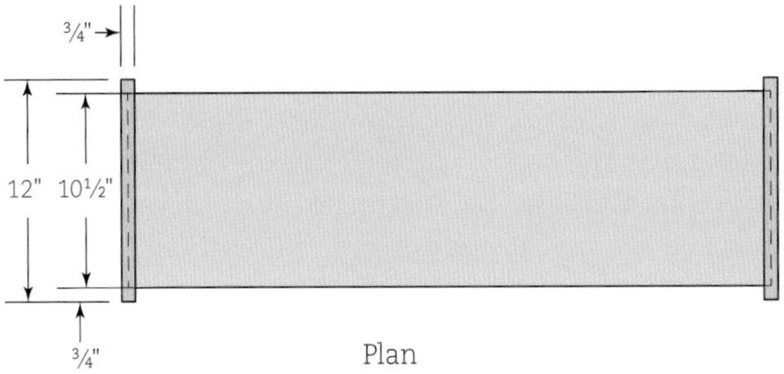

Plan

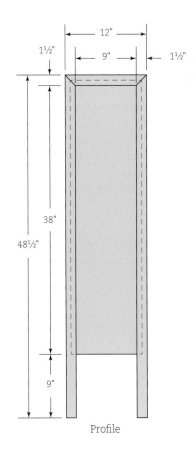

Elevation

Profile

Decorative Drawer

With its prominent placement, the drawer creates a strong focal point for the design of the case – so it's a great place to express yourself.

Do you have a special piece of stock or veneer you've been saving? What about that custom wooden pull you've been wanting to try out? Or Greene & Greene-style finger joints? The drawer's small scale makes it the perfect place for experimentation.

I used some figured maple and created a simple wooden pull, then coved the edges to create a shadow line. Half-blind dovetails join the drawer box, and the plywood bottom is glued into a rabbet.

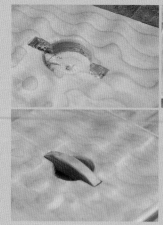

After cutting the drawer front to size, I drilled a clearance space for fingers at the drill press, then chopped a mortise to house the pull. After coving the edge with a router, I glued in the wooden pull.

Tenon the ends of the interior parts with a rabbeting bit (router) or dado stack (table saw), then notch the ends of the boards for the stopped dados. You'll need to round over the tenons or square the dados with a chisel to get the parts to fit.

Cut the Miters

Miters join the case. I used a length of plywood as a fence to guide a large 45° chamfer bit to cut these joints with a router. Simply position the fence along the end of the board, set the bit for a ¾"-deep cut, and rout the chamfer, easing up to the final depth with multiple passes. Cut and miter the case sides now, but leave the ends a little long until after you've dry-fit the case. Doing so allows you to size the pieces for perfect fit.

The frame assembly pieces are also mitered, but these can be cut with a miter saw. If your stock is long enough, cut each assembly from a single board so the grain runs continuously around it.

Rip the parts to width, cut your miters, then cut the legs to final length.

Size the ends of the boards before gluing and clamp in both directions across the joint, taking care that the boards align and the miters stay tight. When the glue is dry, rout a stopped ¾"-wide x ½"-deep rabbet for the case, then square the ends of your cut with a chisel.

Assemble in Stages

Assembling the case is a bit like putting together a jigsaw puzzle. I built the case from left to right in stages. Join the first series of dividers and shelves and let that section dry before adding the next series. Finally, size the miters and glue the ends to the case.

Once the assembly is out of the clamps, level its hardwood faces with a smoothing plane or sander and ease the edges of the boards. Now's a good time to smooth and finish the leg assemblies, too. Glue them to the case, taking care to remove squeeze-out after the glue has gelled, then finish the outside of the case.

With the case and drawer complete, now comes the hard part: deciding what deserves pride of place on your stylish new bookcase.

Assemble the case in stages, building from one side to the other. After the first section is glued up and dry, the second series of shelves and the divider are glued to the first sub-assembly. And so on.

CHAPTER ELEVEN

Monticello's Stacking Bookcases

by Christopher Schwarz

I like to think of Thomas Jefferson's personal library as America's first "bookmobile."

When the British burned down the nation's capitol in 1814, the inferno took with it many of the books owned by the government of our young nation. Lucky for us, Jefferson had a personal library of about 6,700 books – an astonishing accomplishment for the time.

And after some negotiations, Jefferson agreed to cede his entire library at Monticello to Congress for the sum of $23,950. The question was, how to transport 6,700 books from Virginia north to Washington, D.C., with horse-drawn wagons.

Lucky for us, Jefferson was a clever man. He stored his precious library in pine boxes that were designed specifically to travel. While it isn't known if Jefferson designed the book boxes (or "book presses" as they are sometimes called), they do bear the mark of his cleverness.

For when the day came to transport this massive chunk of knowledge, the process was straightforward. Scrap paper was stuffed among the books to protect them, then a lid was nailed over the front of each unit and it was loaded onto a wagon and carted to Washington.

Jefferson's collection of books (which continues to make headlines even today) was the foundation for our Library of Congress. His method for organizing his books (memory, reason and imagination) pushed us into a more modern classification system. Until that time it was common to organize books by height or color.

But What About the Boxes?

While a good deal is known about the books in Jefferson's collection that he sold to Congress, far less is known about the stackable boxes that he used to store his library at Monticello. By examining the written records, officials at Monticello built six bookcases for the museum in 1959 that are a good guess at what would have housed Jefferson's library (though he could have had as many as 20 of these units, if you do the math).

Since the day I started woodworking, I have been concerned about amassing information on the craft. For me, the written word enhances my personal experience

in the shop, and it is a way to stay in touch with the craft while I am on the road, in bed or sitting on the couch.

As my library got out of hand sometime about 2005, I decided I needed to build something to store all my woodworking books. I also wanted something that would allow them to be easily transported when my wife and I leave our house after the kids are off to college, and we launch the next phase of our lives.

And so I became interested in Jefferson's book boxes. I read the original letters that describe how the books were transported. I used the standard measurements

The designer? While we might never know if Thomas Jefferson designed these book boxes, he designed many clever devices at Monticello.

Here are the old dimensions. Jefferson said the bottom cases were 13" deep, the middle cases were 6¾" deep and the top cases 5¾" deep. As to the heights, we can turn to the standard sizes of books at the time (according to the American Library Association). The lower cases were designed to hold "quartos" and "folios." A folio is 15" high x 12" deep. A quarto is 12" high x 9½" deep (the typical size of a modern woodworking book).

The middle cases were designed for "octavos," which are 9" high x 6" deep. The top cases were for "duodecimos," which are 7⅜" high x 5" deep.

So I designed the three different book boxes around these three sizes. As I mentioned above, the lower cases are a little taller than necessary, and the middle cases are a little shallow. But it actually works, and I like the way the boxes step gracefully up my wall.

About the Joinery

I chose to use through-dovetails with mitered shoulders at the corners. This was the same joint the joiners at Monticello used in the 1959 reproductions of the book boxes. I like this joint because it dresses up the front edge of each box with a miter. Also, it is strong and easy to make. Yes, you read that right: easy to make.

You might be wondering if you can cut a mitered through-dovetail joint. The answer is: Yes. It is as easy as a regular through-dovetail, once you let go of your fear of miters and cut the joint freehand and use the joint's natural compression to help you fit it so it's airtight. Of the 24 mitered dovetails in this project, only one is less than airtight. And it was the first one I cut.

The rest of the joinery for these boxes is cake. The ½"-thick backs rest in ½" x ½" rabbets cut into the end pieces and are nailed to the top and bottom of the boxes, which are ½" narrower than the end pieces.

The only other thing to build is the plinth that supports the book boxes. Jefferson's papers don't mention a plinth, but the joiners at Monticello in 1959 built plinths for their cases, and I think it's a fine idea.

The profile I chose for the plinth is a typical late 18th-century foot that you can find on furniture made in both the North and South of the United States. Feel free to select another profile for your plinth, especially if your bookcases will reside in a more modern setting. After all, when old furniture started to look unfashionable, the owners would change the plinth and the hardware to update it. So you can alter your plinth to reflect Shaker, Arts & Crafts or even Scandinavian aesthetics. It's your library.

Building the Shelves

These shelves are 48" long without any center supports. This sounds like a recipe for sagging. But if you nail in your back pieces (which add strength) and use beefy, ⅞"-

for books of the day to help fill in the blanks when it came to designing the three different case sizes Jefferson describes in his correspondence.

Oh, and what was the joinery on these boxes? Who knows. Perhaps the boxes were nailed together, as there were as many as 150 individual book boxes to hold the nearly 6,700 books. But I prefer to think that our third president, who was familiar with the principles of joinery, would insist on something more substantial.

And so, despite the fact that no surviving examples of these book boxes exist, I built each of these units using through-dovetails with mitered shoulders at the corners. The backs are shiplapped and nailed on to the carcases. This approach to building a box is typical for the time, and I bet that my modern book boxes would easily survive a wagon journey from Monticello to Washington, D.C.

A Discussion of Sizes

After researching Jefferson's book boxes and the history of 18th-century publishing, I found that these original book boxes would not be as friendly to the modern library. The largest book box is taller than necessary, and the smaller two boxes are shallower than necessary for some modern titles that are squat. But I decided to build my book boxes to suit old books – you can alter yours as you see fit.

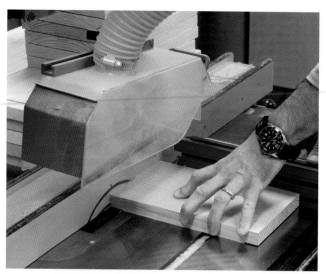

I dressed the concave face of my wide boards with my jack plane then ran them through my powered planer. By jacking one face before planing the other, I avoided having to rip the boards down and re-glue them.

Press the stock down hard to ensure that the cut is consistent across the width of your boards. The dado stack will try to turn your board into a hovercraft. Don't let it. Press down.

thick stock, you will find that your book boxes are nigh on indestructible.

You could get away with ¾" stock throughout without too much of a visual compromise, so don't think that you have to find 4/4 rough stock to build these shelves.

Begin by dressing all your stock to thickness. I was lucky enough to score some Eastern white pine boards of unreasonable widths. So I had to dress the boards for my bottom cases by hand before I could run them through my powered planer.

After dressing my stock to size, I cut a shallow rabbet on the ends of the tail boards. This rabbet is ¹⁄₁₆" deep and the width of the mating pin board. This shallow rabbet makes it quite easy to mate up the two pieces when transferring the marks from my tail board to my pin board.

If I had only a couple boxes to build, I'd make this rabbet with a moving fillister plane. But because I had 28 of these rabbets to cut, I set up a dado stack in my table saw and cut them all using the table saw.

While this might seem like a no-brainer technique, it requires finesse. You need to really press the top of your work hard against the table when making these rabbets. Anything less, and the rotation of the cutterhead will lift the work off the table. No lie.

With all your shallow rabbets cut, you can cut the ½" x ½" rabbets in the inside back edge of the end pieces. I again use a dado stack for this.

Now you can begin to lay out your dovetail joints. This is tricky to explain, but once you cut one mitered dovetail joint, you will laugh loud and hard. It's flipping easy. If you are skeptical, then please give it a try using some scrap first, then you can come crawling ... .

Tail Layout

When you lay out a traditional through-dovetail joint, you will lay out a number of full tails on the tail board. The pin board has full pins – plus half-pins at the ends. Not so with this project.

Because of the miters, the tail joint at the front of the case has one of its corners that mutates into a miter. It looks

Cutting List

NO.	ITEM	DIMENSIONS (INCHES)			MATERIAL
		T	W	L	
LOWER CASE					
2	Ends	⅞"	13"	18"	Pine
2	Top & bottom	⅞"	12½"	48"	Pine
1	Back	⅞"	18"	47½"	Pine
MIDDLE CASE					
2	Ends	⅞"	6¾"	12"	Pine
2	Top & bottom	⅞"	6¼"	48"	Pine
1	Back	⅞"	12"	47½"	Pine
UPPER CASE					
2	Ends	⅞"	5¾"	10"	Pine
2	Top & bottom	⅞"	5¼"	48"	Pine
1	Back	⅞"	10"	47½"	Pine
PLINTH					
2	Ends	⅞"	4¾"	13½"	Pine
2	Front & back	⅞"	4¾"	49"	Pine
1	Interior support, front	¾"	3"	47¼"	Pine
2	Interior support, ends	¾"	3"	11¾"	Pine
4	Glue blocks	1"	1"	4⅛"	Maple
	Moulding	½"	½"	72"	Pine

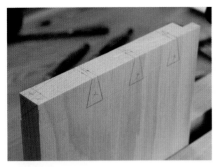

You can see almost all the trickiness here. Note how the tail on the left doesn't go through the face of the board, so it looks like a half-tail. On the right, you can see how the half-tail conceals the rabbet for the back.

Turn your tail board around and cut the front tail on the inside of the corner. It's a 45° cut.

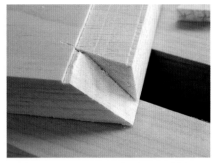

See? Here's the miter at the front, which intersects the sloping tail. Once you see it, you'll get it.

Then turn the board on its side and saw the miter on the front edge. This looks like a complex cut, but just follow the line. It makes sense when the waste falls away.

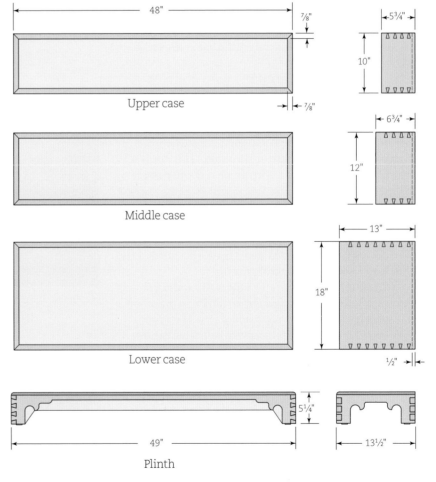

48"
7/8"
Upper case
7/8"
5¾"
10"

Middle case
6¾"
12"

Lower case
13"
18"
½"

Plinth
49"
5¼"
13½"

Elevation

Profile

like a half-pin in one direction and a full tail from another. I know, I know. It seems confusing. Stick with me.

At the rear of each case, I used a half-tail at the back edge so that I could easily conceal the backboards with simple through-rabbets. The half-tail conceals the ½" x ½" rabbet on the inside back edge. As a result, the completed end pieces look a little weird to the traditional eye. But you'll get over it.

So here's how you should proceed: Figure out a tail width at the rear of the case that will hide the backboards and remain strong. Lay out that tail.

At the front of the case, things are a little more complicated. The miter should begin ⅜" from the front edge. So mark a line ⅜" from the front edge of your tail board. Make this mark on the end grain. But don't mark it down the face grain of the outside face of your tail board, which would be typical. Instead, make this sloping tail mark on the inside face of the board. It's weird, I know. But do it.

Lay out the rest of your tail cuts between these two tails, leaving a gap between your tails that is about ⅛" wide at the top.

Now make your tail cuts with a dovetail saw. When you are done with one face, it should look like you have a board with two half-tails at either end. Turn the board around so the rabbeted face is facing you. Take your dovetail saw and make the compound cut at the front of the case that defines the face of the miter. This cut is 45° to the front edge. It looks tricky. It ain't. If you can see the line, you can cut the line.

Now position the board so the front edge of the corner faces the ceiling. Take a miter square (or your combination square) and use it to lay out the miter from the tip of the case to the baseline. When I mark this miter, I use a thin-lead (.3mm) mechanical pencil.

Cut this miter freehand to free the waste at the front of the corner. You'll need to angle the saw at 45° to make this cut. Again, try this once on scrap and you will be a pro.

When that waste has fallen away you can clear out the waste between the other tails. I use a coping saw. But feel free to bang it out with a chisel.

Pin Layout

When the waste is clear, you need to transfer the pattern of the tail board onto the pin board. The shallow ¹⁄₁₆"-deep rabbet makes this a cakewalk. Clamp your pin board upright in a vise. Place the tail board's rabbet on top of the pin board and press the two together. When the two are mushed together, trace the shape of the tail board onto the pin board with a marking knife.

The little mitered section at the front is tough to get a spear-point knife into. Depending on the acuteness of the tip of the knife you can do a fine or a lousy job. Do your best and then "infer" (read: guess) the remainder of the slope with a ruler and a knife.

It's time for tails to meet pins. I have my tail board resting on a scrap to keep it in position as I press its shallow rabbet against the pin board. Knife in the joint. Use light strokes at first, followed by heavier ones.

Here's the completed pin board layout, with the waste marked with "X"s. Clear out the waste between the pins, then cut the miter.

The resulting pin board looks a little more straightforward than the tail board. It's basically a standard-looking pin board with a miter cut on its front edge.

With the lines marked out on the end grain of the pin board, I take the extra step of dropping those lines down the face of my pin board to my baseline. It slows me down, but it's a habit I have yet to break from my first dovetail class.

Slice all the pins with your dovetail saw. But before you remove the waste between the pins, cut the miter at the front of the pin board.

Clamp the pin board on its side and lay out the miter from the tip of the board to the baseline – just like you did with the tail board.

Saw the pins and remove the waste between the pins using a coping saw and chisel. Then saw the miter (on the waste side) freehand. If you are sloppy, clean up the cut a bit to the line with a shoulder plane.

Fit and Slice
When you have the pins and tails cleaned up to your satisfaction, it's time for the fun part: fitting the miters.

Drive the tail board onto the pin board. What is likely to happen is that the tails will seat everywhere but up by the miter. The miter is what is preventing the tail from landing home at the bottom of the pin socket.

When the parts are driven together, they will generate some pressure right at the miter – a good thing. Place the joint on your workbench so the miter faces the ceiling. Take a thin-kerf saw and cut through the miter freehand.

Yes, you read that right. Saw through the miter freehand.

The set of the teeth will remove the excess wood on either side of the saw plate. As you saw, you should feel the wood pinch the blade. Keep sawing. When you reach the bottom of the joint, slide the saw out and the miters should draw closer together. The evidence of this will be that the tail will seat more deeply in the pin socket.

If the miter is tight and the tail is fully seated, you are done. If the tail isn't fully seated, saw through the miter again.

Sometimes the pressure from the joint isn't enough to pull the miters together as you are sawing. If this happens, clamp the joint and then saw it.

Make all the boxes using these techniques. Yes, it takes some time, but by the end you'll be able to make this joint without hesitation, and it's a fine one to have in your arsenal.

The Backs
The backboards for these boxes are nothing more than ½"-thick pine boards that are shiplapped, beaded then nailed on the back of the boxes after the bookcase is finished. You can make your backs now or later.

The Plinth
A traditional plinth looks delicate but will support the entire weight of the book boxes above without any problem. The trick is to design it correctly.

The corners of the plinth should be dovetailed before you cut the scrollwork to create the feet. If you

You can see how the tail isn't fully seated in its socket. The way to fix that is to saw through the miter.

Use a thin-kerf saw and cut right through the miter. The joint might pinch the blade a bit. That's OK. It means the process is working.

cut the scrollwork first, the plinth boards will be too fragile for dovetailing.

After dovetailing the corners, trace your foot design onto the front, back and ends. I drew my shape freehand and it was based on a typical design of the period. Once the shapes are laid out, cut the scrollwork and clean up the saw cuts with rasps or an oscillating spindle sander.

Assemble the four plinth pieces with glue, clamps and lots of care. This is when the pieces are fragile. I destroyed one foot while clamping things together. Luckily, I was able to glue it back on.

With the outside of the plinth complete, work on the inside guts that offer brute strength. I glued a mitered three-sided frame inside the plinth to give it strength. I used 3"-wide boards that were scrap. Really, anything wider than 2" will be fine here.

Once you glue in the mitered frame, flip the plinth over and glue in 1" x 1" maple blocks in the corners. These glue blocks reinforce the corners of the plinth and carry the weight

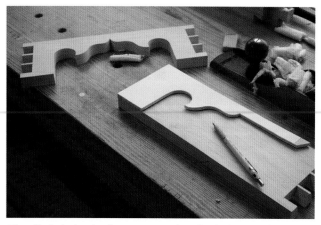

The plinth design is where you can alter the design to suit your house. Like Shaker stuff? Look at Shaker feet and draw something similar on your feet.

I use a block plane to dress the long straight run on the front. But when it comes to the corners, a chisel plane is handy for getting right up against the scrollwork.

This will be covered by the lower case and moulding, so it doesn't have to look pretty. It just has to be strong.

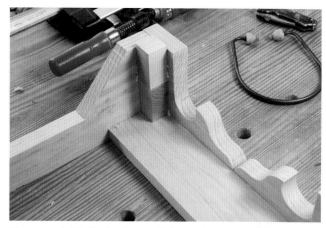

These maple blocks do almost all the work. They are $\frac{1}{8}$" proud of the foot of the plinth and support all of the weight of the book boxes. They also strengthen each corner to protect them from swift kicks.

of the entire bookcase. When made properly, the maple blocks should extend $\frac{1}{8}$" from the bottom of the plinth.

Moulding & Finishing

Trim all the dovetails and prepare the plinth, backs and book boxes for finishing. When that is done, place the lowest book box on the plinth and glue and nail a small moulding around the lowest case. I use a small square ovolo profile here, which matches the period.

To finish the bookcases, I applied two coats of orange shellac, followed by one coat of dull-sheen lacquer. The versions at Monticello are dark brown.

After the finish was dry, I nailed on the backboards using clout nails then stacked the book boxes in place on top of the plinth. To keep the boxes from sliding around, I screwed each box to its neighbor using #8 x 1¼" wood screws. And to keep the bookcase from tipping forward should a toddler attempt to scale it, I attached the whole thing to the wall with an anti-tipping kit.

Then came the best part – loading the bookcase with my woodworking books. These book boxes added 24' linear feet of storage for my books, which have been piling up in my office.

But joy turned to defeat. I have more books than I thought. When loaded, this case holds only half my books. I need to build a second set.

Hmmm, perhaps Jefferson's book boxes were just nailed together.

CHAPTER TWELVE

Bibliophile's Bookcase

by Megan Fitzpatrick

This large case-on-case shelving unit is adapted from similar pieces I've seen in private libraries and in stately homes. I also dug up a few pictures from the Sotheby's and Christie's auction sites, where the form is referred to as a "bibliotheque" (also the French word for library).

Those examples, however, all feature intricate mouldings and fancy corbels and are more adorned than would look right in my less-than-stately 1895 home. I do, however, have 10' ceilings and an embarrassment of books, so while I didn't want fancy, I did want big. So I reconceived the form in a Shaker-on-steroids style – the piece is just shy of 50" wide x 90" high. It will fit in a room with standard ceiling heights, but in case I ever needed to use the top and bottom separately, I installed a solid top for the bottom case so it can stand alone (and with the addition of a cushion, it would make a handsome hall bench).

The size did have me fretting about stock costs, so I culled the "shorts" bin at our local lumber store for lower-priced cherry, and found a nicely figured wide piece for the drawer fronts, as well as sufficient stock for the lower case and all the shelves. The shelves are made of some rather homely boards, but because I added a lip to the front for strength and appearance, you can't actually tell – unless you remove the books and take a close look. I did have to go to the regular-price rack for the upper-case face frame and sides, but I saved money by using poplar for the backboards, which I painted to match the trim in the living room.

Bottom's Up First

First, I cut my parts to rough sizes then surfaced and thicknessed all the stock but the drawer fronts, and glued up panels for the sides, lower case top and upper case top, and all the shelves. I never cut my pieces to final size until I need them – and then I mark cuts using the project as a guide, not the cutlist. No matter how meticulous I am with the measuring, things are never perfect. But, once my pieces are cut to size, I plane and finish-sand as much as possible before assembly because it's hard to maneuver around a piece the size of a New York apartment.

Because I didn't have a 7"-wide piece for the lower rail, or two 49"-long pieces with matching grain that I could glue up, I had to scab on a 4" x 14" piece at each rail end for the curved feet (the downside of parsimony).

I then traced my pattern onto each foot, cut it at the band saw and smoothed the cuts on a spindle sander – but had to resort to hand-sanding where the curve met the flat.

After setting up the mortiser with a ¼" bit, I made a 1½"-wide mortise for the 2"-wide center stile dead in the middle of the lower rail, then moved to the table saw to cut 1¼"-long tenons on each end using a dado stack.

Holding the workpiece took a little thought, because the two feet created a not-solid surface on the bottom edge (a good argument for spending a little extra to make the lower rail and feet out of one board – or at least a solid panel glue-up, and cutting the tenons before cutting out the feet). But no worries – a 3"-long offcut clamped to the sliding table did the trick. I cut each tenon face in two passes, first removing ¾" or so at the end before pushing the end against the fence to remove the remainder of the waste on each shoulder.

The resulting tenon was 6½" wide – on the cusp of too wide to offer sufficient mortise-wall strength – so I split it by sawing out a 1"-wide piece with a coping saw, then chiseled the shoulder flat while removing the remaining waste. I cut 1¼" tenons on the upper rail and center stile at the table saw, marked then cut the mortises on the side rails at the mortiser. After I glued together the face frame and set it aside to dry, it was on to the side pieces.

I marked the curved cutout on each piece, then made the cuts at the band saw. (Note: the apex is not centered; it's ¾" closer to the front.) Because the full dado stack was still in place, I went ahead and added a sacrificial fence, then cut a ¾" x ⁷⁄₁₆" rabbet up the back of each side piece to house the backboards. In retrospect, I should have cut an 11" stopped rabbet, because the backboards don't go all the way to the floor. While the unnecessary 7" portion of rabbet doesn't show, the base would be stronger without it.

I adjusted the dado stack to make a ¾"-wide cut, and made a ¼"-deep dado across each side piece 7" from the bottom (the top edge of the dado is flush with the top of the lower front rail) to accept the web frame, which

Because I had very little extra stock, and not enough with matching grain to glue up a solid panel for the curved bottom rail, I had to scab on the foot piece at either end.

I traced my pattern onto each foot and made the cuts at the band saw.

Because the feet created a non-flat surface, and the sliding table is shorter than my workpiece, I simply clamped a flat piece of scrap to the fence against which I could hold the rail while I made the tenons.

A 6½"-wide tenon is too big, so I split it using a coping saw then chiseled out the remainder of the waste.

The pocket-screwed web frame was glued into the side panel grooves and squared up before I tightened down the clamps.

Again faced with secure workholding problems at the table saw, I used a handscrew attached to the sliding table to support one end, and an stepoff block at the other to safely locate the groove for the bottom fixed shelf.

Be sure you have 1¼" nails in your gun – or if it's loaded with 1½" nails, make sure you angle your shots enough so that you don't blow through the sides. Or keep the nippers handy.

With a big glue-up, it's best to rope a friend into helping. By oneself, it's difficult to tighten all the clamps down quickly without things sliding around – or reach corner to corner should you need to square things up. Or click a camera button from 9' away.

To make a simple crown, angle your stock at 45° to the blade and center the blade on the stock (or cut it just off-center so you have a thicker flat on one edge, if you like that look). Then clamp a long offcut beyond the blade to serve as a fence. Make repeated cuts in each piece of stock, raising the blade a little each time. Stay tight against your fence and to the table. Though I'm not wearing one here, a dust mask would be a good idea.

is joined with pocket screws. I glued the web frame into the dados on each side, squared it up and tightened the clamps. After the glue dried, I glued on the face frame and attached a rail across the top of the back, flush with the backboard rabbets, with pocket screws.

Upper Case

First, I cut the mortises and tenons for the face frame and glued it together (luckily, no one had adjusted the mortiser from when I did the lower face frame). I made it about ⅛" oversized on the sides (as I did with the lower case face frame), so I could flush it easily to the sides later with a flush-trim router bit.

Then it was on to the side pieces, and cutting dados for the bottom and middle fixed shelves. Workholding was tricky here, because the side pieces are 70½" long – well over the edge of the saw table. So, I clamped a hand-screw around the crosscut sled fence, on which to rest the overhanging part. This, however, meant I couldn't use the stop on the sled, so a stepoff block on the fence solved the problem to locate the ¾" dados for the fixed bottom shelf.

I also cut ¾" dados in each side 30⅜" from the bottom for the center fixed shelf, and marked and drilled holes for the adjustable shelf pins. The locations were figured from a graduated shelf progression – but with the remaining three shelves adjustable, it's unlikely that progression will ever be evident.

Stiff Lips

With the sides done, I cut the bottom and middle shelves to size (note that the widths are different; the bottom shelf has no lip), and glued a 1½"-wide lip across the front edge of the middle shelf, leaving just better than ¼" of the shelf's front edge uncovered at each end to slip into the dados.

After the glue dried and I sanded the lip flush, I ran a bead of glue in each side-panel dado, set the fixed shelves in place flush with the front edge of the side, clamped across, then toenailed the fixed shelves in place. Be careful with the angle of your nail gun and the length of your nails. I blew through the side once. OK, maybe three times.

While that glue-up dried, I added lips to the three adjustable shelves, keeping them just shy of either end to make shelf adjustment easier (the face frame covers the shelf ends, so the gap won't show).

Next, I added the face frame, and got a little help clamping it up square – there was simply no way for me to reach corner to corner to pull things into place without assistance. Then, I pocket-screwed a rail at the top edge to which I later attached the backboards.

Topping Things Off

I cut the upper- and lower-case tops to size, and rounded over the edges with #80-grit sandpaper until I liked the way it looked, then progressed through grits to #180 until the shaped edge was smooth.

The lower-case top is attached with L-shaped wood buttons, and has a 1" overhang on the front and at each side; the upper-case top (to which the crown attaches) has a 2⅞" overhang on the front and either side. It's screwed to the back rail, sides and face frame.

A Dusty Crown

I dislike making crown moulding. It is incredibly dusty, and my arms get an unwanted (but not unneeded) work-out pushing ¾" stock at an angle across the table saw blade. But there's no getting around it. So I had to set up the table saw, suck it up (the dust, that is) and get it done. And then there's the sanding. Lots of sanding.

The simplest way to fit the crown is to invert the upper case, then wrap the moulding around the front and two ends. Secure it to the top, sides and face frame with brads.

Put Your Back Into It

My backboards are shiplapped random-width poplar, and in the upper case they're painted. I did cut a chamfer on the front of each for added visual interest – not that it will show when the case is loaded with books.

In the lower section, the backboards are unpainted and have no chamfer – but they do run vertically to match the top. (If you have an 11"-wide piece, you could get away with one board, run horizontally. But your co-workers might snicker at the idea.)

Hidden Storage

Last, I fit the inset drawer fronts and constructed drawers with half-blind dovetails at the front, and through-dovetails at the back. The bottom is an upside-down raised panel slid into a groove (the back edge isn't beveled), then secured to the drawer back with a 1½" shingle nail. I suspect these drawers would have originally housed candles and perhaps paper and writing implements; I'm using them to store extraneous cat toys.

The finish is two sprayed coats of amber shellac (with sanding after each) and a top coat of pre-catalyzed lacquer.

Cutting List

NO.	ITEM	T	W	L	MATERIAL	COMMENTS
Upper Case						
1	Upper rail	¾"	5¾"	47³⁄₁₆"	Cherry	TBE*
1	Lower rail	¾"	3"	47³⁄₁₆"	Cherry	TBE
2	Stiles	¾"	2⅝"	70½"	Cherry	
2	Sides	¾"	11¼"	70½"	Cherry	
1	Bottom fixed shelf	¾"	10½"	48¹⁵⁄₁₆"	Cherry	
1	Middle fixed shelf	¾"	9¾"	48¹⁵⁄₁₆"	Cherry	
3	Adjustable shelves	¾"	9¾"	48¼"	Cherry	
4	Shelf lips	¾"	1¾"	48"	Cherry	
1	Top	¾"	14⅞"	55¹¹⁄₁₆"	Cherry	
2	Crown	¾"	4¼"	54"	Cherry	Rough size
varies	Backboards	⅝"	varies	70½"	Poplar	
Lower Case						
1	Upper rail	¾"	3"	47³⁄₁₆"	Cherry	TBE*
1	Lower rail	¾"	3"	47³⁄₁₆"	Cherry	TBE
2	Feet	¾"	4"	14¼"	Cherry	TOE**
2	Outer stiles	¾"	2⅝"	18"	Cherry	
1	Center stile	¾"	2"	10½"	Cherry	TBE
2	Sides	¾"	12¾"	18"	Cherry	
1	Top	¾"	14½"	51¹⁵⁄₁₆"	Cherry	
2	Drawer fronts	¾"	8"	21¼"	Cherry	Size sides, bottom to fit
varies	Backboards	⅝"	varies	11¾"	Poplar	
Web Frame						
2	Long rails	¾"	2½"	43¹⁵⁄₁₆"	Poplar	
2	Short rails	¾"	2½"	12"	Poplar	
1	Center stile	¾"	4"	7"	Poplar	

* Tenon both ends, 1¼"; ** Tenon one end

BIBLIOPHILE'S BOOKCASE

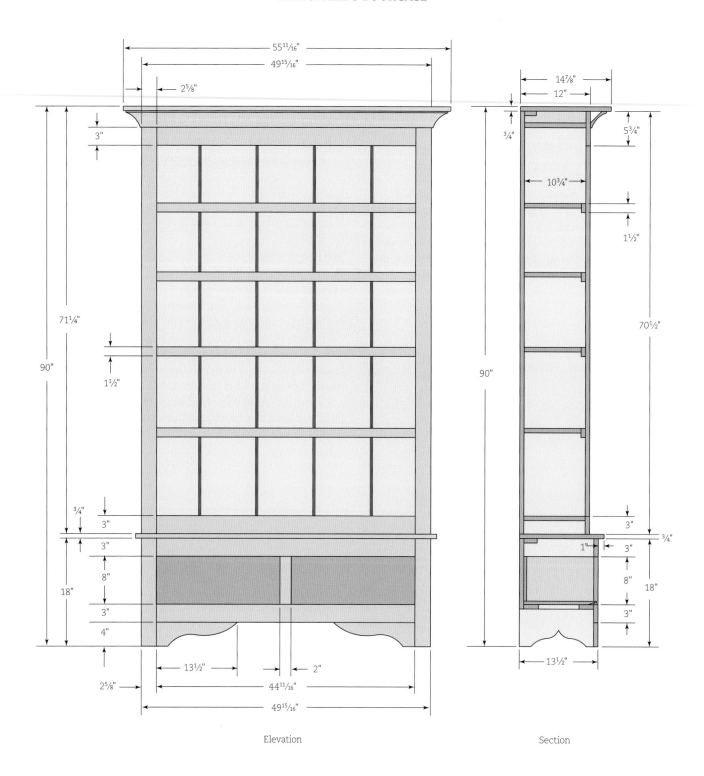

Elevation

Section

CHAPTER THIRTEEN

English Arts & Crafts Bookcase

by Nancy R. Hiller

Some of the most aesthetically compelling pieces of furniture I've seen in the Arts & Crafts style were made by an English company most Americans have never heard of. Between 1890 and 1910, the Harris Lebus Company of London exploited the prevailing fashion in home décor, producing a variety of sideboards, hallstands, wardrobes, washstands and related furniture characterized by simple lines and bold proportions.

Many of these items were production pieces built with a price point rather than handcraft in mind. Yet by virtue of their affordability, these pieces achieved one of the Arts & Crafts movement's central ideals: to make useful and beautiful things available to those of modest means.

While researching an article on Harris Lebus several years ago, I came across a knockout wardrobe. Detail photos revealed less-than-optimal fabrication; the door panels had been screwed into their frames rather than housed in grooves, which resulted in predictable splits. The Gothic-style door and drawer pulls looked like the kind of gaudy hardware that belongs in Hollywood. But the overall look…Wow!

So when I had the opportunity to build a bookcase to go in a bibliophile's home library, I suggested using the Lebus wardrobe as a starting point for the design.

The basic form of the bookcase follows a range of Lebus pieces built with solid-slab side panels glued to front and back legs, without top and bottom rails. The long-grain to long-grain glue-up makes for a perfectly sound connection without any additional joinery.

These side assemblies are connected to each other by mortised-and-tenoned rails at the top and bottom, front and back. The bottom and top are added

The shelf-pin holes are ¾" on center from the inside edges of the legs, spaced 1½" apart vertically. I use a ¼" Forstner bit at the drill press to bore them. For the most harmonious appearance in the finished case, align one or more of the shelves with the lead lines in the glass (and with the muntins, in a mullioned door, for that matter).

Lay out the mortises so the rails and stiles will be flush. I like a 5/16"-wide mortise, and typically leave at least ½" clearance from the top of the leg.

The brackets that wrap the front and sides of the case are seated with sliding dovetails. A router with a ⅜" dovetail bit makes quick work of the slots on the rails. Switch to the router table to cut the slots on the four legs.

later – the bottom supported by wooden cleats, the top attached by metal fasteners or wooden buttons, after the piece's decorative brackets have been installed in sliding dovetail slots.

A paneled back and leaded-glass doors with C. R. Mackintosh hardware complete the picture.

Make the Case and Brackets

When choosing lumber for the bookcase, bear in mind that the most visible features will be the top and bottom front rails, and the rails and stiles of the doors.

Mill and glue up the side panels (and the top, but set it aside for now), then mill the four legs and the top and bottom rails – but don't cut the arch on the front bottom rail until after you have assembled the carcase (removing that much material prior to glue-up would reduce clamping effectiveness). Note: While the sizes for the rails, stiles and panels can be pulled from the cutlist, "verify in field" (direct-measure from the case) the rest of the workpieces rather than relying on the cutlist sizes).

Trim the side panels to final size, then mark and drill for the shelf-support holes. Sand the inside and outside faces now; it would be challenging to sand these after assembly.

Now mortise the legs at the front and back to accept the top and bottom rails that will join the side assemblies to each other.

Cut the matching tenons on the rails to fit; I did this at the table saw using a dado stack. It's critical that the top edges of the front and back bottom rails end up at the same height.

Next, mark out the positions of the sliding dovetail slots for the decorative brackets on the top front rail, then cut them using a router against a clamped-down fence.

Fit the same dovetail cutter into your router table, setting it up so the height of the cut will be precisely the same as the depth of the slots you just cut in the top front rail. Set the fence so that the cutter is centered in the width of the leg, and set a stop so the slot will be approximately the same length as those in the top front rail. Absolute precision here is not that important because you can finesse the fit by hand later if necessary.

Make a mark on the outside face at the top of each leg to ensure that you cut the slots in the correct place, then cut a slot in each of the four legs. If you have dust collection you can do this in one movement; if not, carefully pull the leg back and allow the dust to clear, then push the leg forward to the stop to complete the cut.

Although it's not strictly necessary with brackets that are decorative rather than structural, I cut my bracket blanks so that the grain runs diagonally. Leave the blanks oversized, because the long mitered edges will help ensure accuracy on the router table. (If you run the grain diagonally, scribe the shoulder line of the dovetail

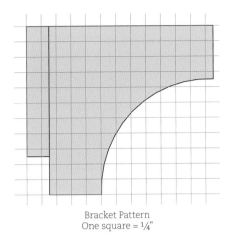

Bracket Pattern
One square = ¼"

To cut the dovetails on the brackets, scribe the baseline to reduce tear-out, then run the blank over the router table. The bit height is the same as that for the leg sockets; you'll need to adjust the fence to center the dovetail on the bracket.

Set a stop to align each bracket for matching cuts as you square the end.

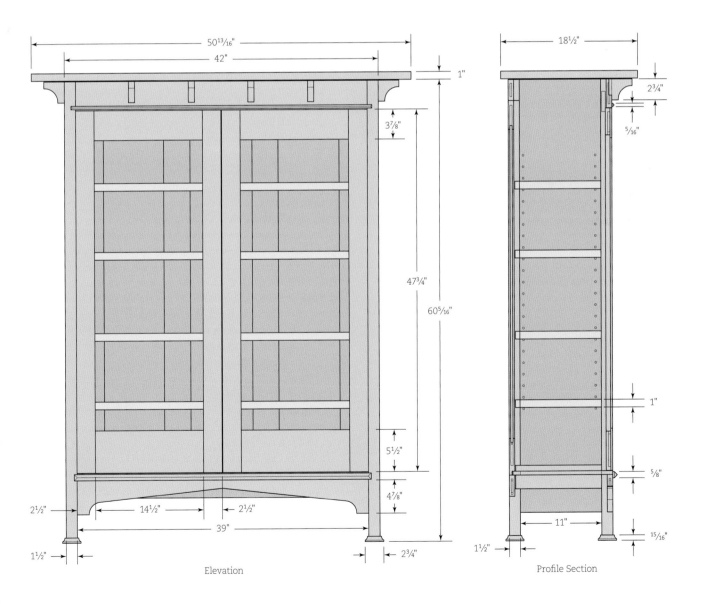

Elevation

Profile Section

on the face where the cut will be going against the grain to avoid tear-out.)

Next, cut the bracket ends square. If you do this on a power saw, you'll need two stop settings: one for the height, and another for the width which includes ⅜" for the dovetail.

Cut off the dovetails up to the shoulder line of their slots using a tenon saw.

Finally, mark the radius for the arch on each blank, cut it at the band saw, then sand. To expedite the sanding of eight brackets, I rigged up a custom tool using an empty cat food can with sticky-backed sandpaper around it, and chucked it into my drill press. (You can, of course, use a spindle sander.)

Glue Up

Because the side panels are butt-glued to the legs without any locating joinery, you need to hold these parts in pre- cise alignment during glue-up. Cut two ³/₁₆"-thick spacers at least as long as the side panels to make the reveal consistent (apply wax to the spacers if you're worried about glue squeeze-out sticking them to your panels). Be sure to glue up the sides on a flat surface; any deviation may alter the reveal. Apply glue to both panel edges, then line up the top of the panel with the tops of the legs.

When the glue in the side assemblies is dry, glue up the frame. Tape a piece of scrap over the dovetail slots in the legs to protect the slots from damage by the clamps. Sight across the top rails to check for racking, then across the front to check for twist. Check the diagonals across the front and top.

Now make a routing template (I use ¼" plywood) for the Tudor arch (refer to the rail pattern on page 93). Cut the arch in the lower rail with a jigsaw, clamp the pattern to the rail one side at a time, then clean up the arch using a top-mounted-bearing pattern bit.

Bottoms Up

Turn the case upside down and make the two-part feet. The blanks for the coved portion are ¹¹/₁₆" thick, 2½" square. Cut the coves on a router table using a ½" cove bit, cutting the end-grain first so the long-grain cuts will remove tear-out. The bases are ¼" x 2¾" squares. Glue and pin the parts together with the coved piece centered on the foot.

Center each composite foot on a leg; you can do this by eye — the overlap is small. Tack them in place, then drill for and attach two countersunk screws to prevent rotation.

Take care when standing the case upright to avoid damaging the feet. Now cut the top to size.

Use traditional wooden "buttons" or metal fasteners to hold the top on the case. If using buttons, you will have to rout or chop mortises near the top of the sides, front and back rails; if using metal attachment hardware, you can cut slots at the requisite height using a biscuit jointer after the case has been assembled. In either case, set the height of the slots so there is a space of about ¹/₁₆" to ⅛" between the top edge of the case and the top of the fastener to ensure a positive pull.

After fitting the top and its attachments, remove it and set it aside for now.

The carcase bottom will be supported by the front and back bottom rails, and by cleats running from the front to the back legs.

Start by cutting cleats to fit between the front and back legs, then mark the inside corner of the legs on the cleat at front and back. Scribe the distance between the inside corner of each leg and the inside face of the carcase side (it should be about ½") on the cleat and cut a notch with a backsaw or at the table saw. The rear notch cut should be offset about ⅛" toward the front to leave additional room for movement of the side.

Cutting List

NO.	ITEM	T	W	L	MATERIAL	COMMENTS
		DIMENSIONS (INCHES)				
2	Side panels	¾"	11"	56⅝"	Oak	
4	Legs	1½"	1½"	59⅜"	Oak	
1	Top	1"	18½"	50¹³/₁₆"	Oak	
4	Feet, cove portion	¹¹/₁₆"	2½"	2½"	Oak	
4	Feet, base	¼"	2¾"	2¾"	Oak	
1	Front top rail	¾"	3¾"	41½"	Oak	*1¼" TBE
1	Front bottom rail	¾"	4⅞"	41½"	Oak	*1¼" TBE
2	Back rails	¾"	2¾"	41½"	Oak	*1¼" TBE
8	Brackets	¹³/₁₆"	2¾"	3⅛"	Oak	**
1	Bottom	½"	13⅝"	40⅛"	Oak	
2	Bottom cleats (under)	¾"	1⅜"	12⅜"	Oak	
2	Bottom cleats (over)	¾"	1⅜"	11⅝"	Oak	
1	Beveled trim, top	⁵/₁₆"	¹³/₁₆"	39¾"	Oak	
1	Beveled trim, bottom	⅝"	⁷/₁₆"	40¼"	Oak	
4	Shelves	1"	11⅝"	40"	Oak	
2	Back stiles	¾"	3¾"	49⅛"	Oak	
1	Back top rail	¾"	3¾"	32½"	Oak	
1	Back bottom rail	¾"	4¾"	32½"	Oak	
2	Back vertical dividers	¾"	3½"	41⅝"	Oak	
3	Back panels	⁵/₁₆"	8⅞"	41⅜"	Oak	
2	Keeper strips	¾"	¾"	42"	Oak	
4	Door stiles	⅞"	2½"	48"	Oak	
2	Door top rails	⅞"	3⅞"	17"	Oak	*1¼" TBE
2	Door bottom rails	⅞"	5½"	17"	Oak	*1¼" TBE
6	Glass keeper strips	¼"	⁵/₁₆"	48"	Oak	†
1	Door stop	½"	2⅝"	45⅝"	Oak	

*TBE = tenon both ends; **Includes ⅜" sliding dovetail on back; †Thickness is approximate

Long strips of ³⁄₁₆"-thick material hold the panels in the correct alignment as you glue the side panels to the legs.

Pads over the dovetail slots for the brackets protect them from clamp damage as you glue and clamp the carcase.

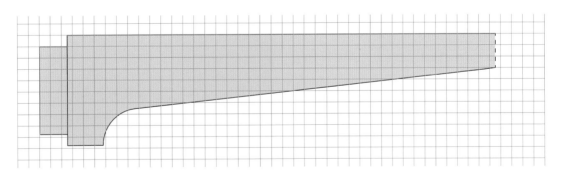

Rail Pattern – left side
One square = ¹⁄₂"

Drill a ³⁄₈"-diameter hole in the notched part at the back to allow the carcase to expand and contract, then glue and screw the cleat in place on the front leg, taking care to make the top face flush with the top edge of the front rail.

Mark the position of the hole on the back leg, drill at the center for a #6 screw, then screw the cleat in place on

the back leg using a ⁵⁄₃₂" x ¾" fender washer and a pan head screw. Repeat on the other side. The washer spans the hole, which is quite a bit larger than a #6 screw, to allow for movement.

The ½"-thick bottom will sit flush with the front face of the cabinet; trim will cover the joint between these parts. Measure the distance from this face to halfway

A ½" cove and slightly larger base combine to create an eye-catching bottom detail to the feet.

You can use metal connectors as I did, or wooden buttons to connect the top to the carcase. Either way, offset the slots in the case sides by 1/16"-1/8" so the top pulls down tight.

Pull the proper length and notch location from the carcase, not from the cutlist.

A fender washer transfers the tension between the fillet and side panel across the 3/8"-diameter hole that allows the side to move freely, and provides a solid surface for the screw head.

through the thickness of the back rail and rip the bottom to this dimension.

Crosscut the bottom to the full interior width of the carcase and notch it around the legs. Sand the bottom, then glue it in place on the front rail only (to allow for expansion and contraction toward the back).

Now cut and notch upper cleats to sandwich the bottom in place and keep it flat. Shape the front to avoid a clumsy look – I cut the same radius as I used for the brackets – and fasten the top cleats in place as you did with the lower ones.

So why go through what seems like more trouble than simply setting the bottom in dados? This down-and-dirty approach (I learned it years ago in a professional cabinet shop) actually makes life easier, particularly on large case pieces such as this one.

The ½" stock reduces the overall weight slightly, there are no dados to cut, and there is one less piece to juggle as you apply clamps to a carcase glue-up. But of

With the back panel held in place, pencil a line where it meets the case bottom. Then, cut a 3/8"-deep rabbet (half the thickness of your back rail) to that line.

course, feel free to approach the bottom in a traditional manner if you prefer.

Back it Up

I made a paneled back that fits inside the opening, without rabbeting the case. The back is joined with pegged stub tenons in a ½"-deep groove with floating panels.

You could opt for a plywood or ship-lapped oak back, but I think the paneled back adds an elegant touch.

Measure the height of the interior opening at the back and cut the stiles to this length, then use these dimensions to calculate the lengths of the top and bottom rails and vertical dividers.

You can avoid a small gap behind the shelves by rabbeting the panel edges so they're flush with the back's frame on the inside of the bookcase. (Because I bought 4/4 stock for these panels and bookmatched them, I made my panels $^5/_{16}$" thick; this resulted in a ¼" gap behind the shelves, which is negligible in a case designed for book storage.)

Fit the back into the opening and mark the horizontal line where it hits the bottom of the case on the interior of the cabinet. Rabbet the bottom rail of the back panel so that it will fit over the bottom of the case with its back face flush with the back of the legs.

Now, with the back set in place, measure for the thickness of the "keeper strips" to which you'll secure it.

To determine this, measure the distance between the inside face of the back and the inside face of the legs – it should be about ¾" – so that the strip will be flush with the front of the legs. Cut the strips to length and glue them in place.

What you're basically doing here is creating a glued-on rabbet – it's simpler than rabbeting the legs to accept the back, and – if you choose strips that match the grain in the legs – no one will ever notice in the back of a bookcase.

After the glue dries, secure the back to the strips with brass screws. (I use four or five on each side).

Now glue the arched brackets into their slots, taking care to make their tops level with the top of the case.

Beveled Trim

Many pieces of Arts & Crafts casework produced by Lebus feature bevels as a decorative element – on the inside edges of door rails and cornices, or to frame sections of casework. I incorporated bevels here in the form of trim above and below the doors; I varied the dimensions to produce proportions typical of a Lebus piece at the turn of the 20th century.

Leave your trim stock overlong until you have cut the bevels on the table saw. Rip one side with your blade at 45°, then reverse the cut to bevel the other side. Note: These cuts will leave a small flat at the edges.

Now cut a 45° bevel on one end, then lop approximately ⅛" off the end to match the long flat of the table saw bevels. Determine the final length (add ⅛" for the flat on the other end), then replicate the bevel there.

Glue and pin the beveled trim onto the face of the cabinet, leaving an ⅛" reveal between each piece of trim and the nearest edge of the top and bottom rail respectively.

Make the Doors

Although you could rabbet the backs of the doors with a router after assembly to accept the leaded-glass panels, the method I use is more traditional for glazed doors and leaves a clean shoulder at the inside corner.

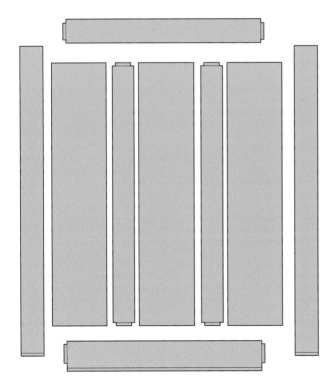

Back – Exploded View

Set the blade on the table saw to 45° and rip one side of the trim, then the other. And, of course, use a push stick for this operation.

Mill the door rails and stiles now, as well as enough extra stock to use for test cuts on setups.

On the inside of all the pieces, cut a ⅜"-wide x ⅝"-deep rabbet (it must be deep enough to accommodate the thickness of the zinc channel in the glass panels). Then use the rabbeted stiles and rails to guide the layout location of the ⁵/₁₆"-wide x 1¼"-deep mortises.

Cut tenons on the table saw, setting the height of the cheek cuts with a piece of scrap with the mortise chopped all the way out to one end.

Set the table saw fence to produce a full-length tenon – the full mortise depth of 1¼" – on the cheeks for the face side of each rail, but for the cheeks that face the interior of the cabinet, reset the table saw fence so the back shoulder of the tenon will fill the groove.

To cut the haunches, leave the table saw fence at the same setting, but raise the dado blades to a height of ½" using the same principle as you did for the case joinery.

Once you're satisfied with how everything fits, glue up the doors.

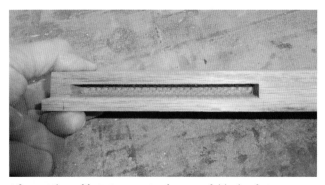

After cutting rabbets to accept a glass panel, it's simple to see where the mortise needs to be laid out and cut.

Show the rail to the stile to mark the location for the stepped shoulder that will fill in the rabbet.

Door Catches

The tall doors should be fitted with catches at the top and bottom. You could certainly use brass ball catches, but I used rare-earth magnets.

Because I've had trouble with magnets exerting too strong a pull when mounted on a door's face – something you really don't want with a leaded-glass panel in a tall door – I mounted them in the top and bottom rails.

First, drill holes for the magnets on the top and bottom of the door stile using a Forstner bit.

Mark the position of the magnet on the cabinet floor and top rail, then drill.

Don't recess the magnets completely; leave them flush or just a little proud, depending on the size of the gap around your doors. They need to touch in order to catch.

As the final touch, attach a small piece of oak to the rail at the top behind the doors, to serve as a stop.

—NH

Get Hinged

The type and installation of the hinges for this piece diverge from much of 20th-century English convention. Most of the casework I encountered in my training and work in England was built with fixed-pin butt hinges mortised into the door alone – not mortised into the surrounding cabinet frame.

But because the doors for this bookcase are relatively large and heavy (which is why you need three hinges per side), I used removable-pin hinges, mortising them into the case as well as the doors to relieve some of the stress on the brass screws.

Fit the doors in their openings, then chop mortises in the door stiles for the hinges. (I typically lay out the hinge location by going no more than ½" above or below where the rails meet the stiles.)

Set the doors on shims to create a small gap at the lower edge, then mark the positions of the hinge mortises on the face of each corresponding leg. Chop or rout the mortises in the legs. Now test-fit the doors with their hinges and adjust them until they hang well. Then remove them and get ready to finish.

The Big Finish

The finish I use here produces a classic Arts & Crafts look, but without the danger of ammonia fuming.

First, sand the entire piece to #180-grit then remove the dust. Apply a coat of TransTint Honey Amber dye at the ratio of 1 tablespoon of dye to 1 pint of distilled water.

Using a foam brush, apply the dye liberally with the grain, working quickly to avoid lap marks. Go over each section with a lint-free cloth to even out the dye before you move onto the next area.

After the dye has dried completely, scuff-sand the raised grain with #320-grit sandpaper. Remove the dust, then apply a coat of Minwax Early American stain using a foam brush. The stain will continue to bleed out of the pores, so wipe periodically with a clean cloth over the next couple of hours to remove any excess.

Allow the stain to dry overnight, then apply a coat of amber shellac.

If you're going to apply a topcoat such as oil-based polyurethane, use dewaxed shellac to promote adhesion. Use a high-quality bristle brush and apply the shellac quickly with the grain to minimize lap lines. You can adjust the color or mimic signs of age with a gel stain glaze, in which case you'll want to wait at least overnight before applying a topcoat.

Don't forget to apply a coat of shellac on the underside of the top and floor so that all surfaces are sealed (I used Zinsser Bulls Eye SealCoat).

A final going over with paste wax will produce a low-luster, satin-smooth finish that's easy to renew with additional wax in the future.

I made my own leaded-glass panels, using directions available online and from various publishers. (The learning curve was steep, and the finished product less than perfect, but I find the panels quite attractive and serviceable.)

You can, of course, use plain glass, or have a glass artist make leaded panels for you.

Install the glass panels in their rabbets, then cut thin strips of wood that tuck into the rabbet to hold the glass in place. Miter the corners, then pin the strips in place, sinking the brads into the side of the rabbet (where there is no glass to avoid). Now attach the top and rehang the doors.

Here's the case after the coat of amber shellac. (Note: Don't panic after the dye and stain coats – you won't get a good look until after the shellac.)

I mixed Old Masters' Dark Mahogany and Dark Walnut gel stains to get the color I wanted, then added swipes of finish in crevices and corners to mimic age.

The final touch is to install the door pulls – which I do with the doors hanging because it allows you to get them exactly even. The ones shown in the opening photo (from Horton Brasses) are in the Mackintosh style, and come close to the hardware on original Lebus pieces of this vintage.

Sources

Rejuvenation
rejuvenation.com or 888-401-1900
6 Ball-tip cabinet hinges #C7685 BA, $25/pair

Horton Brasses
horton-brasses.com or 800-754-9127
2 Mackintosh vertical drop pulls #AD-4065 DA, $41.50 ea.

Rockler
rockler.com or 800-279-4441
12 Top fasteners #34215, $2.99/pack of eight
4 Rare-earth magnets, $3/8$" dia. #32907, $11.99/pack of 10
4 Magnet cups, $3/8$" dia. #39783, $8.99/pack of 8
4 Washers for $3/8$" magnets #38348, $6.99/pack of 10

Jamestown Distributors
jamestowndistributors.com
or 800-497-0010
#6 slotted-head brass wood screws, $1 1/4$" long #FBRWSFH6X11/4, $12.18/box of 100
#6 slotted-head brass wood screws, $1 1/2$" long #FBRWSFH6X11/2, $13.76/box of 100

Delphi Glass
delphiglass.com or 800-248-2048
3 Lead came, $1/4$" x 72" #5584, $6.95 each
3 Zinc channel, $1/4$" x 72" #5601, 4.95 each
Solder, flux and tools for making leaded glass panels

Homestead Finishing Products
homesteadfinishingproducts.com
or 216-631-5309
TransTint Honey Amber Dye #6001, $18.50/ 2 oz. bottle

*Prices correct at time of publication.

CHAPTER FOURTEEN

Barrister Bookcases

by Glen D. Huey

Almost everyone likes the look of barrister bookcases. But what makes them so appealing? I think there are a number of characteristics that make the barrister design popular and enduring.

First is that the individual units of the case stack together. And because they are separate units, they can be arranged in any desired height configuration to fit any area of your home or office.

Second, they are elegant as well as functional. The wood-framed glass doors, when lowered, protect your books or other valuables from moisture and dust – not to mention those tiny pudding-laced fingers of the little ones. They also allow you to look through the glass for a specific item without the undo stress of operating the doors. In the open position, with the doors raised and slid back into the case, you have easy access to those leather-bound sources of knowledge.

Third, as you will see, we rethought the construction so these cases can be built with the easiest techniques – without sacrificing any classic design elements. These are the easiest barrister bookcases you will ever build.

We decided to build a stack of three units – each identical in construction and design, with one slightly different in height. There are two larger units for over-sized books and special keepsakes, and one that is slightly shorter in height. Those, along with the top and bottom units, add up to the appropriate design for our bookcase needs.

Your set can be created with only one unit, or it could be a stack of five, along with the top and bottom sections. (More than five units is unwieldy and potentially unstable.)

One Panel Chops into Three

We wanted the grain on each case side to be consistent from top to bottom as we stacked our individual units. This is a matter of aesthetics, not a necessity. (I'm sure somewhere during this case's lifetime, the units will be stacked without regard to the grain.)

What is a necessity, in order to get the units to stack without problems, is to make the width of each unit equal in size. This is best accomplished by starting with

one large glued-up panel of the correct width that is then crosscut into the appropriate lengths.

Once the sides are milled according to the plan, there are three rabbets that need to be cut in each side panel. One rabbet goes at the top and bottom of each side panel. Those rabbets are for the full-width case bottom

Using the widest setting on a dado stack along with a sacrificial fence is the best choice for creating rabbets for these case sides. This will ensure that the cut clears the waste entirely.

Raising the blade height is the only adjustment needed to cut the backboard rabbets. The front edge of this side looks as though it is raised from the saw top because of the previous rabbet cut.

Creating the groove for the door pins to ride in is the most exacting step of the process. A plunge router with a guide fence makes it short work. Check the layout before routing.

There are pin locations at both the top and bottom that act as guides for the doors. Use the drill press for this step – unless you've a steady hand and good eye.

and the front and back rails at the top. You also need a rabbet at the back edge of the side panels that will house the backboards. That rabbet hides the backboards when viewing the bookcase from the side.

A dado blade is the best choice for cutting the rabbets. Install a sacrificial fence, set the blade for the widest cut (at least ¾") and position the blade below the saw top. Adjust the fence to the blade so that ¾" of cutting width is exposed and with the blade running, slowly raise the cutter to a height of ⅛". With this setting, a single pass over the blade will create the ¾"-wide x ⅛"-deep rabbets at the top and bottom edge of the side panels.

Next, again with the blade moving, raise the height to ⁷⁄₁₆". This is to create the rabbet for the backboards. They fit into a ¾"-wide x ⁷⁄₁₆"-deep rabbet. If you are trying to keep the grain aligned, as we have, you need to determine the front edge of the bookcase prior to

crosscutting the individual side panels into smaller sections. Or, choose the best edge of your stock for the front face at this time and cut the backboard rabbets into the opposite edge.

Your Groove is Important

Creating the groove in which the doors slide is the most difficult task involved in building these bookcases – but all it takes is a plunge router with a guide fence and a ¼" upcut spiral router bit.

Positioning this groove is the trick. It needs to be located correctly from the top edge of the sides, so the guide fence of the router becomes key. Set the fence so the router bit plunges into the side with 1⅛" of material between the top edge and the groove. The ¼" cut will then be perfectly set for the placement of the centered brass rods in the bookcase doors, and it builds in the

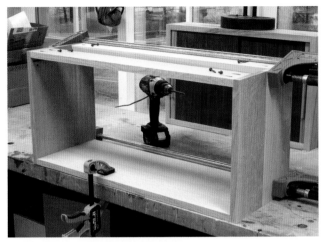

Assembling the boxes is a matter of 14 pocket screws. Clamping the box ensures that it will be square. The opening in the top is for the adjoining catch rail on a second unit.

The catch rail is fastened to the box bottom. It is important to properly align the piece to fit the other units.

The catch rail for the top unit rests inside the end rails. To keep the rail from sliding downward as the screws are installed, rest the piece on a block cut to the correct size.

necessary ⅛" spacing so the top edge of the door does not bind when opened.

Next, you need to find the starting or stopping point of the cut depending on which side you're working. On each right-side panel you'll plunge at the front edge and finish the cut through the backboard rabbet. On the left-side panels you'll begin coming through that rabbet and complete the cut by stopping at the correct location and removing the bit from the work surface. Attacking the groove this way registers each cut off of the top edge of the side panels and makes the best use of the guide fence.

The location that you need to stop on is ⅜" in from the front edge of the sides to the beginning of the routed groove. Where did this number come from, beside the plan? The ¼" brass rods that are used to hang the doors

are located in the center of the ¾"-thick doors. The outer ¼" of door stock along with the design feature of the ⅛" offset of the door to the front edge of the case adds up to that exact location.

With the setup and location locked in, rout the $5/16$"-deep grooves into the sides as shown in the picture at right.

The doors will be held in position toward the front with two brass rods per side. The top rod is centered 1¾" from the top edge of the side and in 1" from the front edge. These two rods act as a pivot for the sliding door.

The second rod location is pulled from the bottom edge of the sides and is also set at a measurement of 1¾". It too is located 1" in from the front edge. This rod placement gives the door something to close against while holding the door parallel to the case front when closed.

Assemble the Box

Mill to size and thickness the material for the top-front rails, rear rails and the catch rails, as well as the bottoms. You can get away with using a secondary wood for the rear and catch rails, as we chose to do, because these pieces will not be seen as you view the bookcase. All pieces connect to the sides with pocket screws.

Cut three pocket-screw holes on the worst face of the bottoms, leaving the best face for the inside of the piece. Position a hole at 1½" from each edge and one that is centered across the bottoms. The rails used for the top also attach with pocket screws. Place two holes at each end of both rails.

Now you are ready to assemble the boxes. Position the bottom on your bench and match the two sides to the bottom, making sure that the bottom fits into the shallow rabbets. Next, slide the top rails in place – the oak at the front and the secondary wood at the rear.

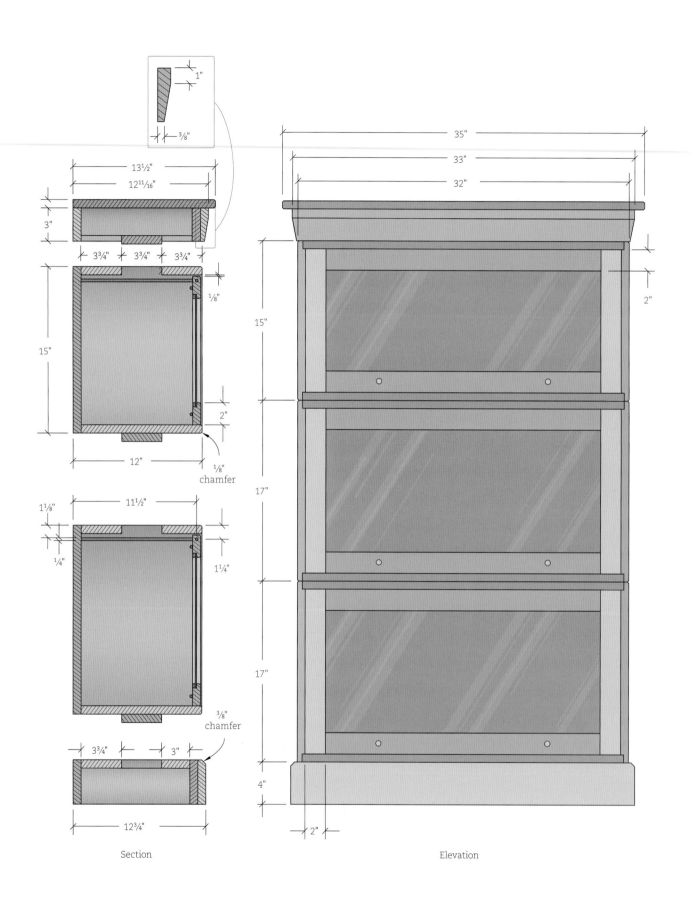

Section

Elevation

The 3" rail in the base unit is toward the front while the wider rail is held to the back. Each rail is not only connected to the frame sides, it is also attached to a center support.

The chamfered base moulding is fit to the base frame on three sides. The secondary wood of the frame is hidden when the bookcase is stacked.

These rails fit into the rabbets at the top edge. Add clamps as shown above then attach the rails to the sides with the screws. Flip the box then add the screws to attach the bottom.

With the box set on its top, position and attach the catch rail to the bottom. Align the piece off of the front edge of the unit and center the rail from side to side. Each rail lines up with the inside face of the side, not the edge of the rabbet area. Attach the rails to the bottom with wood screws.

Creating the frames for the top and base units is next. We found that building the frames and then attaching the mouldings was the best way to approach this part of the project. It also allowed us to use secondary wood for these hidden areas.

Each frame starts with the assembly of a box. The end supports receive the pocket-screw holes and are attached to the rails through that connection. Also, while you have the pocket-screw jig out, add a number of holes to the top frame that you'll use for attaching the top.

With the narrowness of the frames, you should arrange the pieces so the screws are to the outside of the unit. The drill, with the square drive installed, is too large for the inside of the frame. You should also attach the center support, the piece that runs from front to back and is centered along the width of each frame, through the outside with four #8 x 1¼" wood screws.

From this point the construction of the frames differs. In order for the top and base units to fit the design of the bookcase, the top unit must have a catch rail while the base unit receives a front and back flat rail.

The catch rail of the top unit fits between the frame's side rails, with a ¼" extending beyond the side rails, and attaches to the center support with two #8 x 1¼" wood screws.

Make sure that the catch rail is aligned to fit into the top rails of any of the bookcase units – they are all consistently positioned, making them interchangeable.

In the base unit the front and rear flat rails are set flush with the top edge of the frame and attached using the pocket-screw method. Remember that the front rail is only 3" wide, whereas the rear rail is 3¾". Each of these flat rails also attaches to the center support with #8 x 1¼" wood screws.

The mouldings are next. Mill the material for the crown moulding, the base moulding and the bookcase top to size and thickness. The top edge of the base moulding has a ⅜" chamfer. Cut the edge with a router equipped with a chamfering bit, then fit the pieces to the base. Because there is a solid frame backing the mouldings you can nail the pieces in place with brads. Add a small bead of glue at the mitered corners as you assemble the mouldings for added strength.

Make the Crown Moulding

The crown moulding is a bit more complex than the base moulding. It begins with a cut at the table saw. Tip the blade to 10° and position the fence so that the blade exits the stock about 1" down from the top. This will leave about ⅜" of material at the bottom edge of the stock. This setting will need to be fine-tuned at your saw. Run the cut for both pieces of stock – one for the front and one piece that is crosscut into the two ends.

I elected to make a pass over the jointer to clean up the saw marks on my mouldings. Set a light depth of cut and be sure to use push sticks. If you choose not to use the jointer you can sand the moulding face smooth. Once the piece is cleaned and sanded it can be attached to the top frame.

While the setup is involved, the ripping of the crown moulding is straightforward. Just make sure to have a push stick handy.

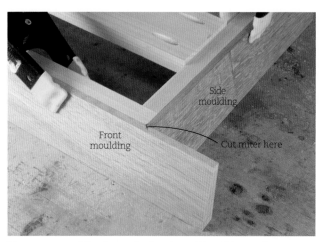

The crown moulding is attached to three sides of the top frame. Miter the corners and add a small amount of glue to reinforce the area. Brads will affix the pieces to the frame.

Side moulding

Front moulding

Cut miter here

I work counter-clockwise around the unit to get an accurate fit when wrapping mouldings. This allows for easy marking of cutlines as well as easy positioning of the cuts at the miter saw and it allows me to make my mitered cuts without changing the angle of the saw. Cut and fit the first mitered corner and clamp the

The cutting of the crown moulding can leave saw kerf indications and burn marks. A quick run over the jointer knives works best to clean the face.

pieces to the frame. Slide the third piece, with its end cut square, to meet the back of the front crown piece and mark the top edge on the front moulding.

At the miter saw, align the mark with your blade (saw angled to the right) and make the 45° cut. With the top edge up it is easy to match the blade to the layout line. Now to cut your final miter, simply place the end piece at the saw with the top edge pointing down while the face side is out and make the cut. The angle of the saw doesn't change and the cuts are correct. This is also how I would cut the first mitered corner.

Place the top unit, with the moulding now applied, onto the bookcase top, centered from side to side and flush to the back edge of the top unit. Use pocket screws

Complete the work on the top unit by attaching the moulded frame to the case top. Pocket screws are quick and easy.

to attach the frame to the top then set the completed top unit aside.

The Doors are a Snap

The only easier method that could be used to build doors would be a flat-paneled door and that wouldn't give us the glass panels that we need for these cases. The secret for these doors is accurate cutting of the pieces.

Rip the material to the required width then set stops at the saw to allow for accurate cutting of the required lengths. If the pieces are all cut to the same sizes (two matching sets of the rails and stiles per door) two things will happen – one, the doors will be square when assembled and two, the assembled doors will correctly fit the openings of the boxes.

Cut the stiles to be ³/₁₆" less than the opening of the box and the rails to be 4⅛" less than the total width of that opening. This will build in the appropriate reveal around the doors.

These doors are also assembled with pocket screws placed in the rails, and the location of the holes is important. If the hole is too close to the outside of the rail, as you drive the screws there is potential to crack the end of the stiles. If the hole is set too near the interior of the rails, as you rabbet for the glass, you have the possibility of cutting into the screw area. The best location is at ⅝" from both edges.

With the pocket-screw holes cut you can now assemble the doors. Place a clamp over the intersection of the two pieces, a rail and a stile, and drive the screws. Work the four corners of each door in the same manner.

Positioning the pocket-screw holes in the door rails is important. Too close to either edge can cause problems. Don't forget to add glue at the joint.

The ⅜" x ½" rabbet for the glass and the retainer strips requires that you climb cut a portion to eliminate any tear-out.

Squaring the corners left rounded from the router bit is a job for the chisel. It works best to begin with a cut across the end grain and to then take small cuts with the grain, removing the waste.

Adding a small bevel to the edges of the piece will help hide the joints between the separate units. This edge work also allows the doors to flip up and slide back into the case without binding.

Drilling jig

Door

Aligning the holes for the doors to pivot becomes easy work with the use of this shop-made jig.

you're likely to have areas, especially in quartersawn white oak, that will splinter and tear out. To remedy this you must climb cut during a portion of this process.

Start by climb cutting the first ⅛" of the rabbet then reverse the routing procedure and complete the rabbet. By having a small shelf of routed area from climb cutting, the removal of the balance of the waste material will shear off at that point and prevent most tear-out.

To complete the rabbet you'll need to square the rounded corners left from the router bit. Use a straight-edge to continue the lines to reveal the exact corner and use a sharp chisel to bring the rounded corners to square. Clean the corners until you're level with the bottom of the rabbet.

Before moving forward now is the time to create the small bevel on the edges of the doors as well as the edges of the boxes themselves. Chuck a chamfer bit in a router and set it to cut ⅛" and run the profile around the doors outside edge and along the top and bottom of the boxes, including both sides and the front.

Each door edge, at the top of the door, needs to have a hole drilled to accept the short brass rod (available at any hardware store) on which the door will hang and travel in the groove as it is opened. A shop-made jig is just the trick to complete this step quickly and accurately.

Build the jig using a scrap of the cutoff material from your door pieces. Locate the center of the piece, which will be ⅜" from the edge, and also mark a line that is ⅜" in from the end. At that crossing is where you need to drill the ¼" hole completely through the block. Use the drill press because you need the hole to be straight.

Next, add two pieces of Masonite, or other thin plywood-type material, to both sides of the block. To use the jig, slide it over the long grain of the stile, keeping the ⅜" space toward the top edge of the door. Add a clamp to hold the jig and drill the hole using the jig as a guide. Set the drill bit to cut to a depth of ¾".

Drill two holes per door, install a 1" piece of brass rod using no glue (we need to be able to remove them over the remainder of the project). Once the rods are in place you can test the door to the opening. If you have a problem it will most likely be binding at the top or bottom.

In either case you will need to remove a sliver of material to allow the fit. This can be done at the jointer or with a plane. Both solutions require you to work carefully around the end grain. All that's left is to cut the plywood pieces that comprise the backs of the individual units and mill a number of pieces to use as the glass retainers from some scrap.

Finish as Easy as the Project

This finish technique was developed by Robert W. Lang. If this method had been around years ago when I was working with oak, I would have built many more projects

Rabbeting the doors for the glass and glass-retainer strips is another router operation. Install a rabbeting bit, set for a ⅜" rabbet, and cut the interior of the frame. It is necessary to position the door hanging over the edge of your table or bench so the bearing screw does not rub the bench.

If you try to make the entire cut by running the router in the standard manner, into the bit rotation,

Cutting List

NO.	ITEM	DIMENSIONS (INCHES) T	W	L	MATERIAL	COMMENTS
2	Case sides	3/4"	12"	50"	QSWO*	Cut to length shown in drawing
3	Bottoms	3/4"	11 1/4"	30 3/4"	QSWO*	
3	Top front rails	3/4"	3 3/4"	30 3/4"	QSWO*	
3	Top back rails	3/4"	3 3/4"	30 3/4"	Poplar	
3	Box catch rails	3/4"	3 3/4"	30 3/4"	Poplar	
2	Top frame rails	3/4"	3"	32"	Poplar	
2	Top frame sides	3/4"	3"	10 1/2"	Poplar	
1	Top frame center support	3/4"	2 1/2"	10 1/2"	Poplar	
1	Top frame catch rails	3/4"	3 3/4"	30 1/2"	Poplar	
1	Front crown moulding	3/4"	3"	36"	QSWO*	
1	Side crown moulding	3/4"	3"	26"	QSWO*	Makes both sides
1	Case top	3/4"	13 1/2"	35"	QSWO*	
2	Base frame rails	3/4"	4"	32"	Poplar	
2	Base frame sides	3/4"	4"	10 1/2"	Poplar	
1	Base frame center support	3/4"	3 1/4"	10 1/2"	Poplar	
1	Base frame front flat rail	3/4"	3"	30 1/2"	Poplar	
1	Base frame back flat rail	3/4"	3 3/4"	30 1/2"	Poplar	
1	Base moulding/front	3/4"	4"	36"	QSWO*	
1	Base moulding/sides	3/4"	4"	26"	QSWO*	Makes both sides
6	Door rails	3/4"	2"	26 3/8"	QSWO*	Rails for three doors
4	Door stiles/tall	3/4"	2"	15 1/16"	QSWO*	Stiles for two doors
2	Door stiles/short	3/4"	2"	13 1/16"	QSWO*	Stiles for one doors
9	Glass retainer strips	5/16"	5/16"	28"	QSWO*	For three doors
1	Short unit back	3/4"	14 7/8"	31 7/16"	QSWO*	Plywood
2	Tall unit back	3/4"	5/16"	31 7/16"	QSWO*	Plywood

* QSWO=Quartersawn White Oak

from this hardwood. You will not find an easier finish anywhere that I know of.

To begin, don't waste a huge amount of time sanding. I know you like the sound of that! Bring the piece to #120-grit with the random-orbit sander and finish sand by hand using #150-grit sandpaper. Done! Now you are ready to stain the bookcase.

The staining process continues in the easy category. Rag on a coat of Olympic oil-based "Special Walnut" stain. Apply an even coat and allow it to sit for 15 minutes before wiping any excess away. That coat needs to dry for 24 hours before moving on.

The barrister bookcase gets an Arts & Crafts look with the simple finishing method described for this project. It works great for oak – both white and red.

Next up is one coat of Dark Walnut Watco Danish Oil. Apply this in the same fashion as the stain. Rag a coat onto the stained bookcase and allow that to cure for 15 minutes, then wipe away any extra oil with a clean rag. In this process the oil acts as a toner that will even the shading as it adds color to the project. Again, let the oil coat dry for a day.

The rags used in both of the previous steps can become a fire hazard if not disposed of properly. You can lay the rags out on the floor of your shop or put them into a bucket of water. Combustion is a result of these rags thrown into a pile either in the trash can or a corner of the shop. Always dispose of rags properly.

The final step in the finishing process is to apply a coat of amber shellac. Can you guess how this is applied? You bet: Rag it on. Keep a wet edge on the wide-open areas and on any other areas simply coat them. That's it. Once the shellac is dry (the next day) add a coat of paste wax after knocking down any nibs with a non-woven abrasive pad.

The Finishing Touch

Attach the plywood backboards to the back of the units with screws after the finish is complete. All that is needed is to run four screws, one at each corner, through the pieces and into the unit bottom and the rear rail of the unit top. Use a countersink and wood screws for a professional look.

Installing the glass and knobs will complete the bookcases. Have 1/8" glass cut to fit the openings of the doors and fit a glass-retainer strip around the inside of the rabbet holding the glass in place.

The knobs are like the rest of the project; simple and elegant. What would finish this project better than a simple brass knob? Find the location and drill a pilot hole to make installing the knobs a snap. A bit of wax on the threads will ensure easy installation.

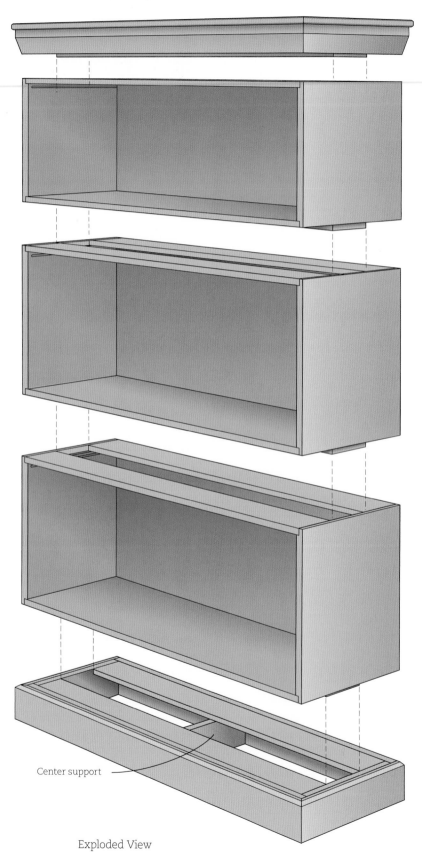

Center support

Exploded View

With the finish complete, an easy way to install the glass for the doors is with matching retainer strips. They are cut and fit then attached with a 23-gauge pinner.

Sliding the doors into the boxes is the last step before filling the bookcase with your books. Slide the door into the case on a slight angle to the front, lift the brass rod on the side toward the rear of the case into the groove and position the other rod to move into the groove as you bring the door square to the front.

Lift the door so it is perpendicular to the case and slide it to the rear of the case. Holding the door up to the top of the unit, install ¾"-long brass rods into the remaining holes. Your barrister bookcase is ready to use.

The great thing about this barrister bookcase design is that as your collection grows, and you know it will, so can your bookcases. You can add to the existing stack or start another bookcase. They are easy to build and adding to the stack is something you will enjoy.

No glue is used to hold the brass rods in place. They can be removed if the door should ever need to be taken out of the bookcase.

Sources

Horton Brasses
800-754-9127 or horton-brasses.com
6 • knobs, ¾" semi-bright #H-42
Call or check website for pricing.

CHAPTER FIFTEEN

Floor to Ceiling Bookcase

by David Radtke

If you're bursting at the seams with books, here's a bookcase that maximizes space, fits any room, and uses lumberyard mouldings.

A Flexible Design

This bookcase is designed without a back or base unit to make it easier to fit into any room. You can build around vents and outlets by simply shifting a standard (the upright piece supporting a shelf). This only affects the length of the shelves, which is not difficult to change in the Cutting List, page 114.

Without a base or back, will the bookshelf be sturdy? Sure, because hidden steel pins made from lag bolts go right into the floor and hold the standards rigid.

Are your floors and walls out of square? Not a problem. We've engineered this project to work even if your room is a bit out of kilter. The mouldings are applied individually to each standard and cover any gaps resulting from uneven floors or walls.

1 Use shortest height for measurement

Measure the height and width of your wall. Note the locations of all receptacles, switches and vents. If they're in the way, modify our design by relocating a standard and changing the length of the shelves.

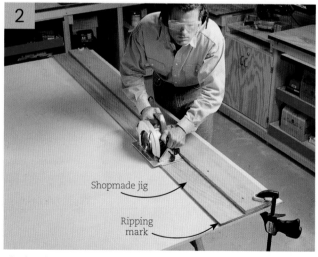

2 Shopmade jig

Ripping mark

Rip the plywood into strips for the standards. Although you can use a table saw to make these cuts, you won't have to struggle with a bulky sheet of plywood if you use a circular saw and a simple cutting jig.

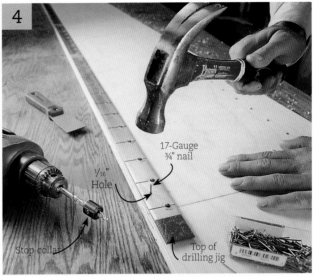

Make a foolproof, durable jig to drill accurate holes for the shelf-support pins. Drill ¼"-dia. holes into a 1¼" x ⅛" x 6' piece of aluminum or steel bar stock (available at hardware stores).

Nail the jig to the plywood through four small holes drilled along the jig's length. Identify the top of the jig with paint or tape, then align the top hole with a line 84" from the plywood's bottom (see Fig. A). Drill ¼" holes ½" deep through each of the jig holes using a stop collar to limit the hole's depth. Remember, the end standards don't require holes.

Easy Moulding

A large built-in requires a lot of moulding, so we've chosen a mixture of classic shapes that you can buy through a lumberyard or home center. We special-ordered the maple mouldings for our bookcase, but if you build yours from oak or pine, moulding to match is readily available. We'll show you how to modify one moulding to make an impressive cornice, complete with dentils (Photo 10).

This bookcase blends right into your room reusing your existing baseboard moulding. Simply cut your moulding and reinstall it between the standards.

Size and Cost

We designed this bookcase to fit into a typical room with an 8' ceiling and at least 8' of wall space, something like a typical bedroom you may want to convert to a library or home office. You can enlarge this bookcase simply by adding standards.

We spent about $600 on materials for the bookcase shown here. The optional ladder and hardware cost an additional $700 to $1,200, depending on how fancy it is (see Sources, page 117). Before you make sawdust, check out our advice on Planning Your Bookcase, page 115. Then follow Photos 1 through 15 for the nitty gritty how-to.

Finishing

Finish the standards, moulding and shelves before installation. This keeps spills and obnoxious fumes out of your

Glue 2x4s between the plywood pieces to create the standards. Be sure the front 2x4 is flush with the front edge of the panels and the rear 2x4 is set in about ½". After assembling, scribe the standard to fit the wall, if necessary. The ½" overhang on the back makes scribing much easier.

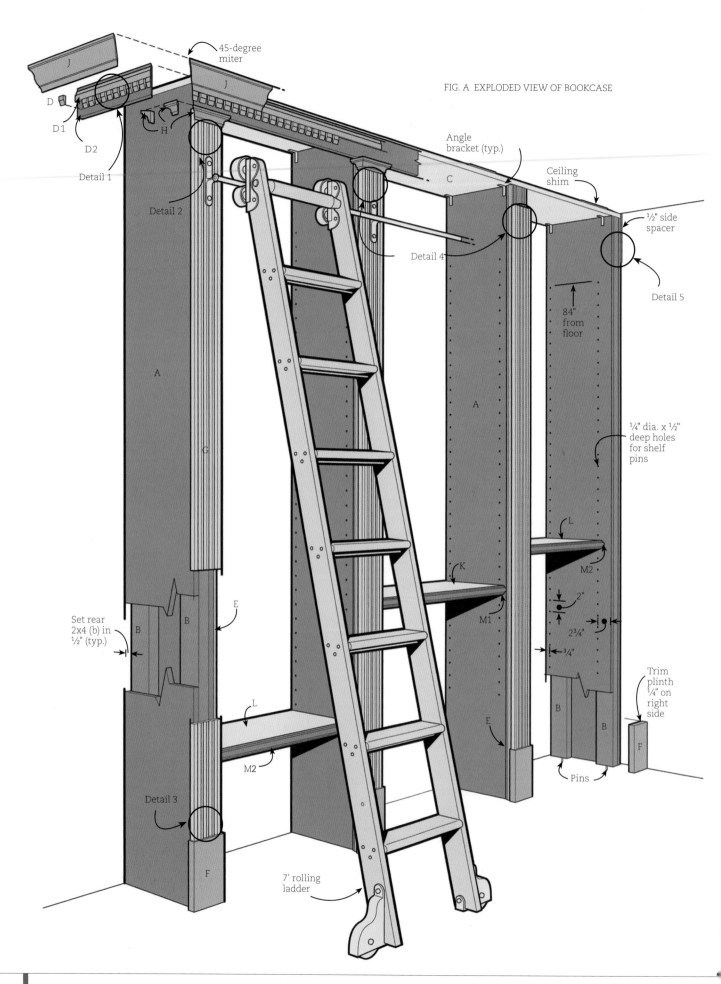

FIG. A EXPLODED VIEW OF BOOKCASE

45-degree miter

J

D

D1

D2

Detail 1

H

Detail 2

Detail 4

Angle bracket (typ.)

Ceiling shim

C

½" side spacer

Detail 5

84" from floor

A

A

¼" dia. x ½" deep holes for shelf pins

G

L

M2

K

Set rear 2x4 (b) in ½" (typ.)

B

B

E

M1

2"

2¾"

¾"

L

M2

B

E

Trim plinth ¼" on right side

B

F

Detail 3

Pins

F

7' rolling ladder

CROSS SECTIONS

Detail 1

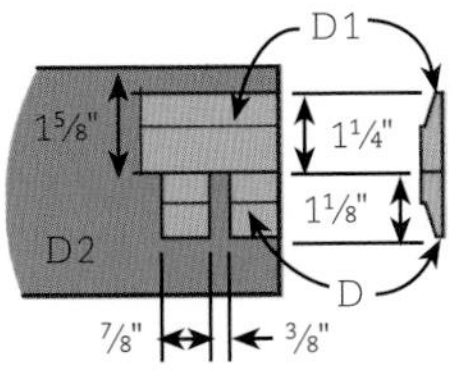
D1
1⅝"
1¼"
1⅛"
D2
D
⅞"
⅜"

Detail 2

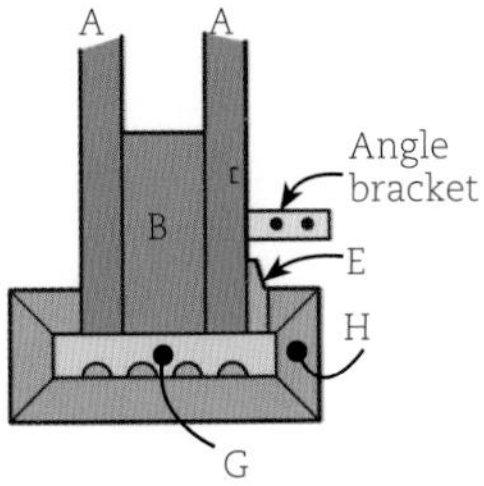
A
A
B
Angle bracket
E
H
G

Detail 3

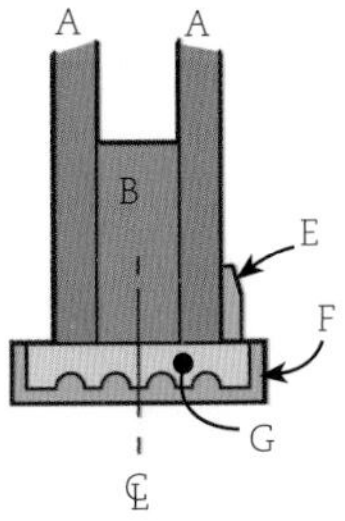
A
A
B
E
F
G
℄

Detail 4

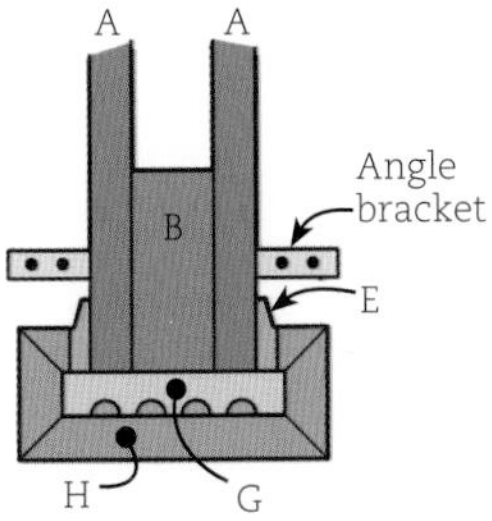
A
A
B
Angle bracket
E
H
G

Detail 5

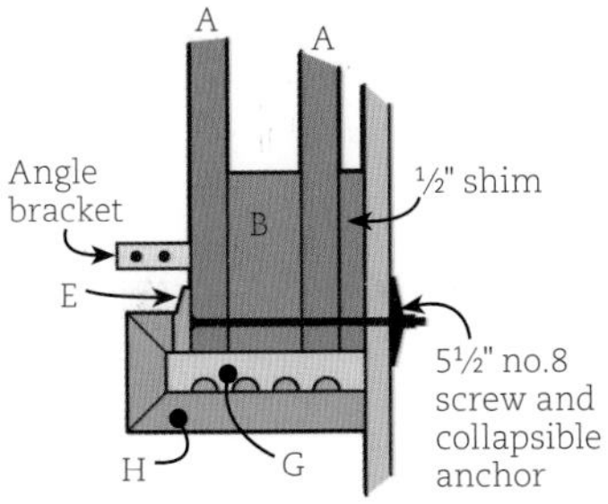
A
A
Angle bracket
B
½" shim
E
5½" no.8 screw and collapsible anchor
H
G

Detail 6

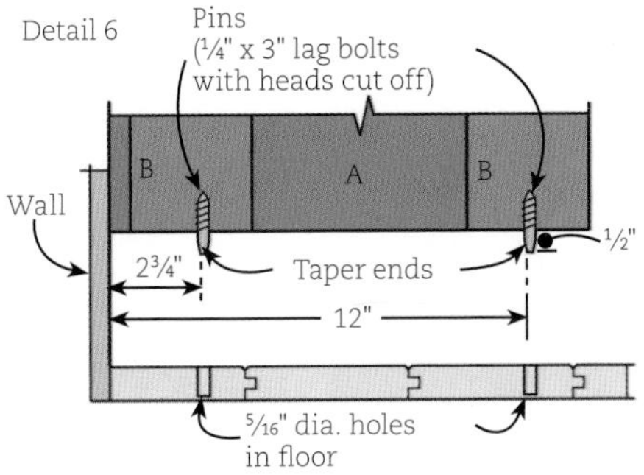
Pins
(¼" x 3" lag bolts with heads cut off)
Wall
B
A
B
2¾"
Taper ends
½"
12"
5⁄16" dia. holes in floor

Detail 7

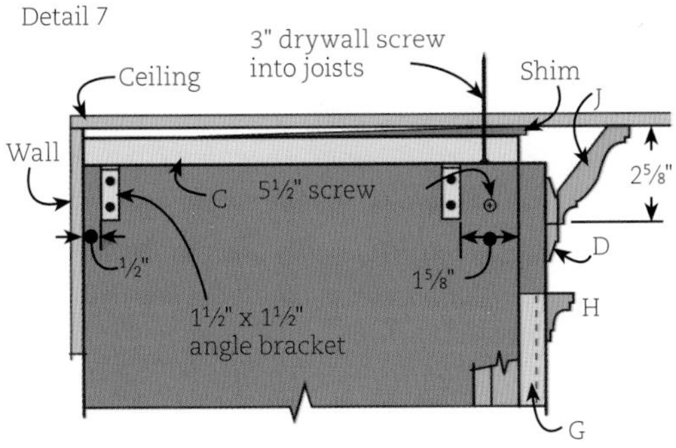
3" drywall screw into joists
Ceiling
Shim
J
Wall
C
5½" screw
2⅝"
D
½"
1⅝"
1½" x 1½" angle bracket
H
G

FIG. B CASINGS AND MOULDINGS

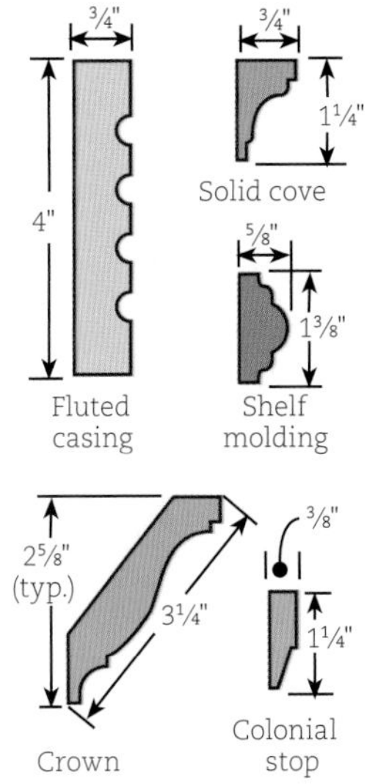
¾"
¾"
1¼"
4"
Solid cove
⅝"
1⅜"
Fluted casing
Shelf molding
2⅝" (typ.)
3¼"
⅜"
1¼"
Crown
Colonial stop

SHOPPING LIST

Item	Quantity	Item	Quantity
¾" x 4' x 8' plywood	5	1¼" x ⅛" x 6' bar stock	1 1½" x 1½"
2x4 x 8' pine	8	angle brackets w/ screws	12
1x2 x 10' pine, for braces	1	yellow glue	1 qt.
1x4 x 10' board, same as moulding	1	¾" x 17-gauge nails	1 pkg.
⅜" x 1¼" x 10' colonial stop	2	1¼" x 17-gauge brads	1 pkg.
⅜" x 1¼" x 8' colonial stop	6	4d, 6d and 8d finish nails	1 lb. each
11⁄16" x 4½" x 8" plinth blocks	4	Minwax wood conditioner	2 qts.
¾" x 4" x 7' fluted casing	4	Minwax No. 245 pecan stain	2 qts.
⅝" x 1⅜" x 8' shelf moulding	7	Minwax satin polyurethane	2 qts.
1¼" x 8' cove moulding	1	Colored putty stick	1
3¼" x 10' crown moulding	1	¼" x 3" lag bolts	8
¼" peg-style shelf brackets	84	Collapsible anchors	4

6

Cut lag
screw

3" Lag
screw

7

Baseboard
removed

Masking
tape

⁵⁄₁₆" dia. hole
locations

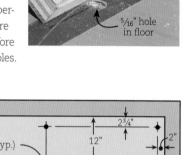

¼" Pin

Taper

⁵⁄₁₆" hole
in floor

Install a pair of pins to hold the bottom of the standard into holes you'll drill in the floor (Fig. A, Detail 6). Make the pins from 3" lag screws. Use a wrench to turn them until the threads are all inside the bottoms of the 2x4s. Then cut off the heads of the screws with a hacksaw and file a slight taper on the bottom of the protruding pin.

Mark the floor locations for the pins on masking tape (Fig. C). Use a framing square as a guide to ensure that the holes are perpendicular to the wall. Be sure to remove the baseboard before you measure and drill the holes.

CUTTING LIST Overall Dimensions: 8' H x 8' L x 14¾" D

PART	QTY.	NAME	MATERIAL	DIMENSIONS	COMMENTS
A	8	Face	Plywood	¾" x 13¾" x 96"	Trim length is 1". less than the distance from floor to ceiling.
B	8	Brace	2x4	2" x 4" x 96"	Same as above.
C	1	Top	Plywood	¾" x 13¾" x 96"	Trim length to fit.
D	a.n.	Dentils	Colonial stop	⅜" x 1¼" x ⅞"	Rip 10-ft. long, 1¼" wide molding to 1⅛" Then cut dentils to length.
D1	2	Filler strip	Colonial stop	⅜" x 1¼"	Cut 10-ft.-long piece to fit.
D2	2	Backer boards		¾" x 3½"	Cut 10-ft.-long piece to fit.
E	6	Molding	Colonial stop	⅜" x 1¼"	Cut 8-ft.-long pieces to fit.
F	4	Plinth blocks		¹¹⁄₁₆" x 4½" x 8"	
G	4	Casing	Fluted casing	¾" x 4"	Cut 7-ft. pieces to fit.
H	a.n.	Cove	Cove moulding	¾" x 1¼"	Cut from 8-ft. length.
J	2	Crown	Crown moulding	2⅝" tall	Cut from 10-ft. length.
K	7	Middle shelves	Plywood	¾" x 11⅜" x 32"	Trim length is ³⁄₁₆" less than distance between standards.
L	14	Outer shelves	Plywood	¾" x 11⅜" x 26"	Same as above.
M1	7	Shelf molding	Shelf molding	⅝" x 1⅜" x 32"	Same as above.
M2	14	Shelf molding	Shelf molding	⅝" x 1⅜" x 26"	Same as above.

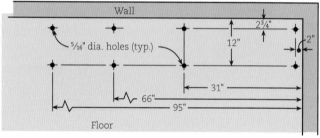

Wall

⁵⁄₁₆" dia. holes (typ.)

2¾"

12"

2"

31"

66"

95"

Floor

FIG. C
LOCATIONS OF FLOOR PINS
(TOP VIEW)

Planning Your Bookcase

This built-in bookcase is easy to enlarge, work around windows, or change in any way to suit your room. Before you buy your lumber, carefully measure your selected site. Take into consideration the height, width and any obstructions unique to your room.

The center section of our bookcase is 6" wider than the two outer sections. This establishes a focal point, and the two side sections provide symmetry. Keep in mind that you can move the standards closer together or add a standard or two to fit a longer wall.

If you move the standards to accommodate outlets or air vents, note that the standards should never be farther than 36" apart. This is the maximum distance for sag-free shelves and safe installation of the rolling-ladder hardware.

Use a level to check for irregularities like a sloping floor or an uneven wall. If they're not too far off, the standards won't need altering. But if your walls and floor are way out of whack, you'll be able to scribe the standards on the backside and bottom, and then cut along your scribe for a perfect fit.

Our bookcase was built onto a wood floor. If you have carpeting, you'll need to pull back the carpet and pad and reinstall them later around the base of the bookcase. And yes, the ladder will roll on carpeting.

8

Top measurement

Temporary brace

Bottom measurement

Receptacles and floor vents are the bane of most built-ins, but not this one. Just locate the standards so they miss the obstacles.

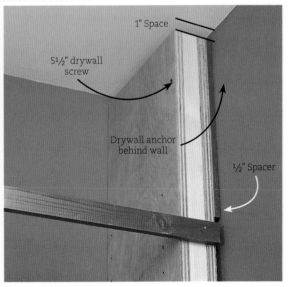

1" Space

5½" drywall screw

Drywall anchor behind wall

½" Spacer

Tip the standards into position. Each standard should be plumb and equally spaced, top and bottom. Start with the standard that goes in the corner, facing the wall (see inset). If the wall isn't plumb, nail shims onto the spacers fastened to the standard's side to compensate. Fasten the standard to the wall with long drywall screws and anchors (Fig. A, Detail 5). Next, tip the second standard into the holes in the floor. Have an assistant hold the standard in place while you make sure it's plumb and the top and bottom measurements are equal. When everything's lined up, lock the standard in place with a temporary brace.

9

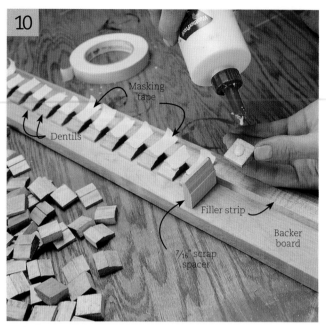

10

Slide the cabinet top over the standards and secure it in place with angle brackets (Fig. A). Shim the gaps between the top and the ceiling. Screw the top to the ceiling joists in three locations using two screws at each location. Note: You may have to use a stud finder to locate the ceiling joists, or install blocks between joists in the attic.

Prefinish all the parts in your shop to keep the mess and smells under control.

Make dentil moulding from Colonial-style stop moulding (Fig. B). You could start from scratch, but this is much easier. First, glue and nail a long piece of moulding (the filler strip) to a backer board. Then cut individual dentils from a long strip of moulding and glue them onto the backer board with a small dab of glue (Fig. A, Detail 1). Use a scrap piece of moulding as a spacer.

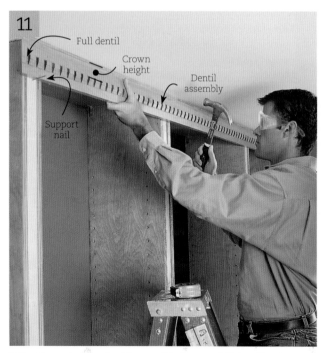

11

12

Miter the end of the dentil assembly. Leave a full dentil at the miter, then cut the assembly to length. Nail it to the front of the standards with 6d finish nails. Maintain a consistent distance from the top of the dentils to the ceiling. This space must match the height of your crown moulding (Fig. A, Detail 7).

Nail molding to the front of the standards with 6d finish nails (Fig. A, Detail 3). Nail the plinth blocks at the bottom first. (Because the plinth blocks are wider than the fluted casing, you'll need to rip ¼" from the width of the block that's against the wall.) Nail the Colonial stop moulding even with the fronts of the standards; then apply the fluted casing.

13

Glue mitered cove moulding to the tops of the fluted casing. The cove moulding should wrap around to meet the Colonial stop moulding (Fig. A, Details 2, 4 and 5).

14 Crown moulding

Nail the crown moulding onto the dentil assembly. Miter each end at the outside corner and butt the other ends against the wall. Use 4d finish nails every 12" and drive them below the surface of the wood with a nail set.

living space. After the bookcase is completely installed, you can touch up any cut ends with stain and fill nail holes with colored putty.

For a blotch-free, even color on this birch, we applied Minwax Wood Conditioner before staining. Then we used Minwax No. 245 pecan stain to blend the maple and birch pieces. Finally, we applied a polyurethane varnish for durability.

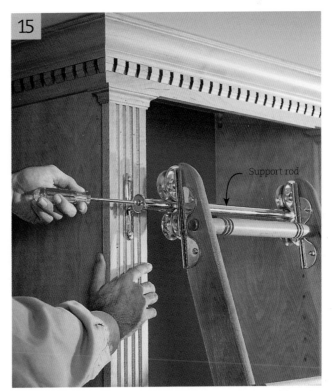

15 Support rod

Optional: Install the rolling ladder hardware to the face of the cabinet according to the manufacturer's instructions (see Sources).

Caution: The ladder is a safety hazard for small children. Adult supervision is advised.

Sources

Rolling ladder and hardware are available from Putnam Ladder, 32 Howard St., New York, NY 10013; (212) 226-5147, www.putnamrollingladder.com. Specify the length of rod (ours is 8') and the height of the finished ladder (ours is 7'). Available in a wide variety of hardwoods. Rolling ladder kits are also sold by ALACO Ladder, 5167 G St., Chino, CA 91710, (888) 310-7040, www.alacoladder.com.

Fluted casing (4") and plinth blocks (4½") are available in a wide variety of hardwoods from Woodharbor Doors & Cabinetry, 3277 Ninth St., Mason City, IA 50401, (641) 423-0444, www.woodharbor.com. Call to order or to find a dealer near you.

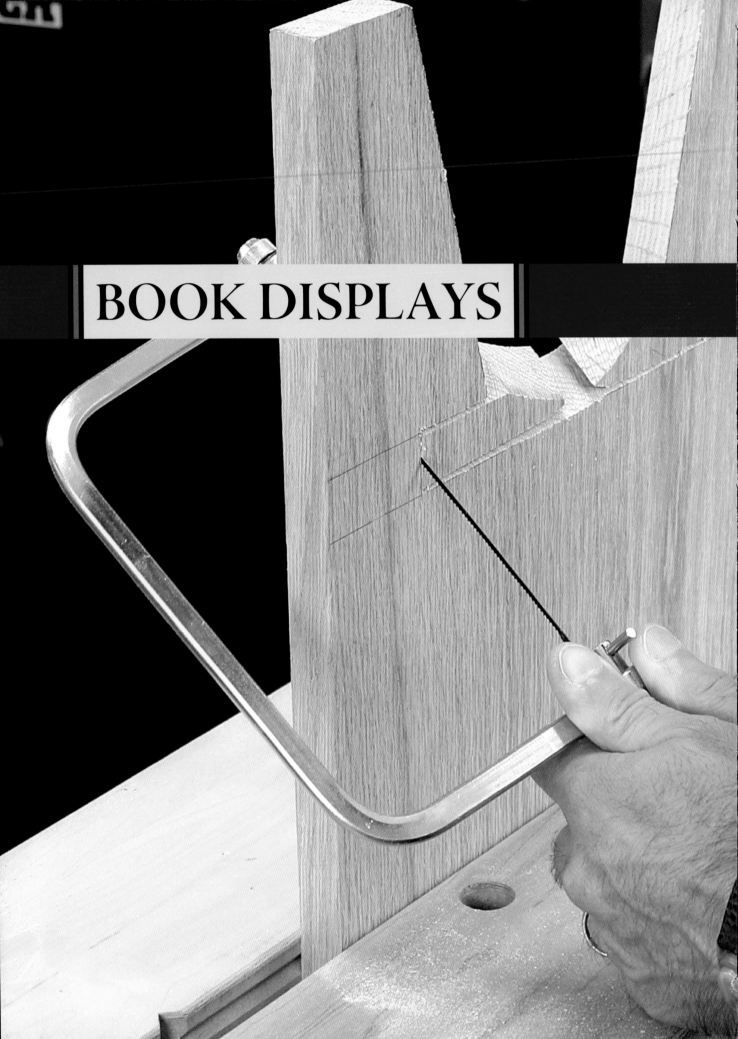

BOOK DISPLAYS

CHAPTER SIXTEEN

Magazine Rack

by Christopher Schwarz

Because you're holding this magazine, chances are you could use a magazine rack by your favorite chair to hold your current crop of periodicals and catalogs.

And because you like magazines, I suspect that you also like books, and you might have need for a stand to hold open your favorite reference book – whether that's a dictionary, "Baking Illustrated" or "Tage Frid Teaches Woodworking."

If you're nodding your head in agreement to either of the above statements, we have one project that can scratch both itches. This simple project has only two parts and they interlock: Slide them together one way

and they make a magazine rack; slide them together the other way and they make a bookstand.

And here's the best part: You need only a handful of tools to make this project. Plus, it's a quick job; I built the version shown here in just a couple hours.

Gather Your Materials

You can find all the materials for this project at the local home center. So with a construction drawing in hand I hit the lumber section. I wasn't happy with the No. 2 pine in the racks. The poplar was an uninspiring purple. But there were a couple promising red oak 1 x 12s. These

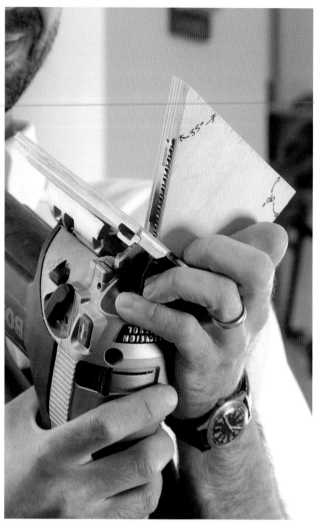

This scrap of wood acts as a reliable way to set your jigsaw's base to 35°. I found a protractor difficult to balance on the base and not nearly as accurate.

were expensive: $40 for a 6' length. But that was enough to make two racks, so I pulled the trigger.

Make a Simple Jig

This project requires you to set the base of your jigsaw at 35° to the blade, sometimes tilted left and sometimes tilted right. To make these changes quickly and reliably, I made a little jig from a scrap. You don't have to make the jig for this project, but it sure makes life easy.

My blade-setting jig was made from a scrap piece of ¾"-thick plywood that was about 3" wide and 12" long. I cut one end at 90° on my miter saw. Then I set the saw to make a 35° miter and cut off about 3" of the plywood. The piece that falls off is the jig for setting the blade.

By placing the jig on the saw's base you can tilt the base to 35° left and right quickly. And you can use the square edge of the jig to return the saw's blade to 90°.

Make Your Straight Cuts

Use the drawing to lay out all your cuts. Then, with the blade set at 90°, make the cuts that define the two feet on one piece and the single foot on the other piece.

Then make the square-shaped cutouts on each piece. Here's how: Drill a couple ⅜"-diameter holes near the corners of the square-shaped cutout. Then use your jigsaw to remove the waste and square up the corners.

Make Your Bevel Cuts

Tilt the jigsaw's base to 35° left and make all the cuts you can with the blade tilted this direction. Then tilt the blade the other direction and make the remainder of the cuts on the two pieces. In the end you'll have some waste hanging onto your work that needs to be removed with a coping saw. It's simple work. If you don't have a coping saw, use a chisel and a mallet to pop out the waste.

Clean up all your cuts with a rasp, file and sandpaper. Then fit the two parts together – you might have to adjust a few edges with a rasp to get a good fit. If the part with the single leg is just a little too thick to fit through the slot in the other, reduce the thickness of the single leg with your block plane until everything fits. Sand all your parts and add a clear finish (or stain or paint).

In our office, we have far too many magazines for this project to be useful to us. So we're going to use it as a stand for our office dictionary, which settles our debates on word usage. But if we ever need a magazine stand, it's just a flip of the pieces away.

You can rotate the blade in its frame with a coping saw to make a tricky cut like this very easy.

Cutting List

NO.	ITEM	DIMENSIONS (INCHES)			MATERIAL
		T	W	L	
2	Interlocking slabs	¾"	11¼"	16"	Red oak

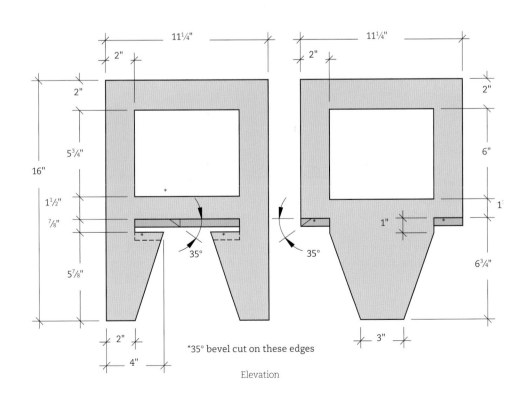

*35° bevel cut on these edges

Elevation

CHAPTER SEVENTEEN

Sliding Bookrack

by Doug Stowe

G ot books? Add a benchtop mortiser and a weekend in your shop, and you're set to create a useful and attractive way to display them. Check it out: Building this Arts and Crafts style cutie, including a template for cutting the mortises, requires only 1 bd. ft. of lumber. That means you can use primo wood, such as quartersawn white oak. And once you've made the template, you can build these bookracks by the dozens.

Cut the Five Parts

Plane the stock to ⅝" thickness and rip the parts to width (A–D Fig. A and Cutting List, page 125). Set aside the rod blanks. Then cut all the remaining parts, including the template, to length on the table saw, using a sled or a miter gauge equipped with a fence and a stop block. The template should be identical in size to the fixed brace (A) and the adjustable brace (B). Sand both braces and the fixed end (C) to #220-grit. This will minimize sanding after the bookrack is assembled.

Cut the Mortises

Create a template that will make it easy to accurately position the pieces for mortising. Lay out the mortises on the template. The rod mortises are spaced 1" from the bottom and ¾" from the edges. The decorative mortises

are 1" from the top, ¾" from the edge and spaced ¼" apart. Install a ½" mortising chisel in the mortiser and set the fence 1" from the bit.

Position the template on the mortiser with the bit centered on one of the bottom mortises. Clamp on a stop block (Photo 1). Then cut a through mortise (Photo 2). Flip over the template, lower the bit into the mortise and clamp on a second stop block (Photo 3).

Use the two stop blocks to cut the bottom mortises in both braces and the fixed end (Photo 4). Complete

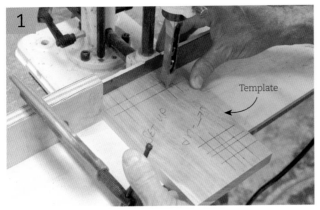

1

Create a template to set up the mortiser. Position the bit to cut the first mortise by adjusting the fence and clamping on a stop block.

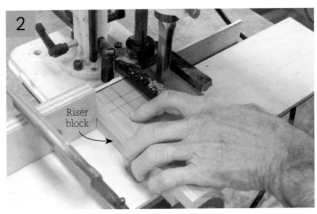

2

Cut a through mortise. Use a riser block to lift the template above the fence so the mortiser's hold-down works properly.

3

Flip over the template and lower the mortising bit into the mortise. Then install a second stop block.

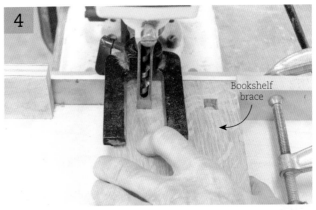

4

Use the two stop blocks to cut the bottom mortises. Cut three-quarters through each workpiece, then flip it over and use the opposite stop block to complete the cut.

each mortise by cutting partway through on both faces. This prevents the splintering and blowout that can occur on the back face when a mortise is cut through from one face.

Turn the braces around and use the same setup and method to cut one mortise at the top – the first decorative mortise. Make sure to position the workpiece against the appropriate stop block when you flip it over to complete the mortise.

Cutting the three remaining decorative mortises in the two braces requires a slightly different approach, because each mortise requires a separate setup. Clamp

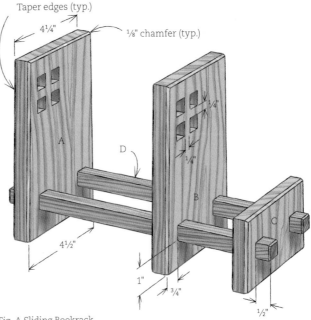

Fig. A Sliding Bookrack

Template

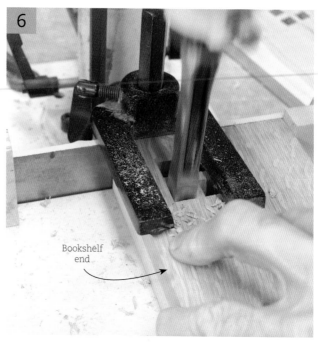

Bookshelf end

Each decorative mortise requires a unique setup. After cutting each new through mortise, flip over the template, engage the bit and install the second stop block.

Use the appropriate stop-block setup to cut each decorative mortise. As before, cut three-quarters through each workpiece, flip it over and use the opposite stop block to complete the job.

on both stop blocks after cutting each through mortise in the template (Photo 5). Then cut that mortise in both braces. Repeat the process to cut the remaining decorative mortises (Photo 6).

Final Shaping and Fitting

Cut $^1/_{16}$" off the bottom of the adjustable brace so it will slide freely as it's moved from one position to another. Taper the outside edges of both braces by hand (Photo 7). Taper both ends of the fixed end on the table saw, using the miter gauge outfitted with a fence and a stop block. Set the miter gauge at a shallow angle (2°–3° from square) to match the tapers on the braces.

Plane the two rod blanks down to fit the mortises. Make sure the rods (D) freely pass through the mortises in the adjustable brace, but fit the mortises in the fixed brace and fixed end tightly enough to be effectively glued. If the rods bind on the adjustable brace, sand them lightly between the points where the fixed brace and fixed end will be glued. Using a chisel to enlarge the mortises on the adjustable brace is a more difficult option.

Slightly chamfer the edges of both braces and the fixed end. Chamfer the ends of the rods, but leave their long edges square.

Assembly and Finish

Before assembly, tape the faces of the fixed brace and fixed end to keep them free of glue. Slide both braces and the fixed end onto the rods – make sure the decorative mortises are oriented correctly. Then use tape to mark the locations of the two fixed pieces on the ends of the rods. Place the assembled rack on a flat surface. Carefully apply glue to the rods and slide the fixed brace and the fixed end into position (Photo 8). Make sure these pieces remain perpendicular. A small amount of glue may squeeze out and puddle where the pieces of tape meet. Use a chisel to remove this glue after it has hardened to a leather-like consistency.

When the glue is dry, remove the tape and sand lightly as necessary. Then apply a finish such as Deft Danish Oil.

Slightly taper all the edges from bottom to top. Reducing the mass at the top helps the bookrack's overall appearance.

8

Apply glue to the rods and then slide the fixed brace and fixed end into position. Tape marks the spot and protects the surfaces from glue that squeezes out.

Cutting List Overall Dimensions: 4½" x 7" x 12"

PART	NAME	QTY.	MATERIAL	TH X W X L
A	Fixed brace	1	Oak	⅝" x 4½" x 7" (a)
B	Adjustable brace	1	Oak	⅝" x 4½" x 7" (a, b)
C	Fixed end	1	Oak	⅝" x 2¼" x 4½"(c)
D	Rod	2	Oak	½" x ½" x 12"

Notes:

a) Taper both outside edges by ⅛", so the top end measures 4¼".

b) Cut ¹⁄₁₆" from bottom after a mortises and tapers have been cut.

c) Taper the ends to match the slope of the braces.

Contributors

Michael Crow is the author of "Building Classic Arts & Crafts Furniture," and "Mid-Century Modern Furniture: Shop Drawings & Techniques for Making 29 Projects."

Megan Fitzpatrick is the editor of *Popular Woodworking Magazine*.

Nancy R. Hiller designs and builds custom furniture at her shop near Bloomington, Ind. Her work has been published in such publications as *Fine Woodworking*, *Popular Woodworking Magazine*, *Fine Homebuilding*, *Old-House Interiors*, *Old-House Journal* and *American Bungalow*. Her web site is nrhillerdesign.com.

Glen D. Huey is a former senior editor with *Popular Woodworking Magazine* and the author of several woodworking books.

Randy Johnson is the former editor-in-chief for *American Woodworker* magazine. He is currently the Chief Operations Officer at ShopBot Tools.

Robert W. Lang is a former senior editor with *Popular Woodworking Magazine* and the author of several woodworking books.

Laurie McKichan designs furniture to be "simple, honest and direct." You can see more of her work at www.lauriemckichan.com

David Radtke is a designer, builder and writer. His work has appeared in *The Family Handyman* magazine and *American Woodworker*. His portfolio includes built-in bookcases, custom furniture, cabinetry, outdoor projects and porches.

Christopher Schwarz is a contributing editor to *Popular Woodworking Magazine* and founder of Lost Art Press, a publishing company dedicated to helping modern woodworkers learn traditional hand-tool skills. He has produced numerous books and DVDs and teaches woodworking around the world.

Doug Stowe is the author of numerous box-making books. His boxes and furniture have been featured in *Woodworkers Journal*, *Woodwork*, *American Woodworker*, *Wood Magazine* and *Fine Woodworking*.

David Thiel is a former senior editor for *Popular Woodworking Magazine* and now works with videos under the Popular Woodworking brand.

Building Bookcases & Bookshelves. Copyright © 2016 by Popular Woodworking Books. Printed and bound in China. All rights reserved. No part of this book may be reproduced in any form or by any electronic or mechanical means including information storage and retrieval systems without permission in writing from the publisher, except by a reviewer, who may quote brief passages in a review. Published by Popular Woodworking Books, an imprint of F+W Media, Inc., 10151 Carver Rd. Blue Ash, Ohio, 45236. First edition.

Distributed in Canada by Fraser Direct
100 Armstrong Avenue
Georgetown, Ontario L7G 5S4
Canada

Distributed in the U.K. and Europe by
F+W Media International, LTD
Pynes Hill Court
Pynes Hill
Rydon Lane
Exeter
EX2 5SP

Tel: +44 1392 797680

Distributed in Australia by Capricorn Link
P.O. Box 704
Windsor, NSW 2756
Australia

Visit our website at popularwoodworking.com or our consumer website at shopwoodworking.com for more woodworking information.

Other fine Popular Woodworking Books are available from your local bookstore or direct from the publisher.

ISBN-13: 978-1-4403-4663-7

20 19 18 17 16   5 4 3 2 1

Editor: *Scott Francis*
Cover Designer: *Daniel T. Pessell*
Interior Designer: *Laura Spencer*
Production Coordinator: *Debbie Thomas*

Metric Conversion Chart

Inches	Centimeters	2.54
Centimeters	Inches	0.4
Feet	Centimeters	30.5
Centimeters	Feet	0.03
Yards	Meters	0.9
Meters	Yards	1.1

a content + ecommerce company

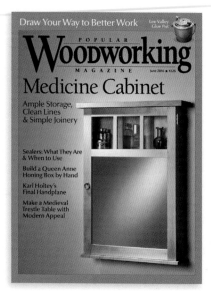
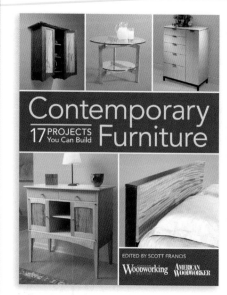

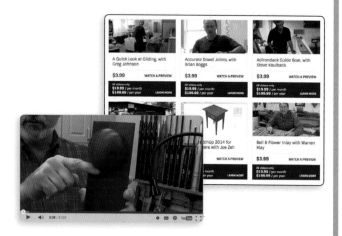